CASTING AND FISHING
THE
ARTIFICIAL FLY

CASTING and FISHING the ARTIFICIAL FLY

By

JOHN W. BALL

DRAWINGS BY PERS CROWELL

The CAXTON PRINTERS, Ltd.
CALDWELL, IDAHO
1981

First printing January, 1972
Second printing December, 1974
Third printing October, 1981

International Standard Book Number 0-87004-217-3

Library of Congress Catalog Card No. 79-140119

Printed and bound in the United States of America by
The CAXTON PRINTERS, Ltd.
Caldwell, Idaho 83605
137356

To those few persons with the courage to crusade for the vital deity of Nature and her creatures.

CONTENTS

FIGURES

CASTING AND FISHING
THE
ARTIFICIAL FLY

INTRODUCTION

I HAVE DISCOVERED that writing an introduction to the following pages isn't easy. Perhaps this may be partly because I have been forced to conflict with a few legends and traditions of long standing, and also because I fear that the average reader anticipates any treatise on fishing to be more relaxing than informative. This one isn't.

If you had lived most of your life in an environment where a lot of nice people still believed the world was flat, yet you felt compelled to teach otherwise to persons searching for facts, you could probably appreciate my problem.

Before anyone can learn, one must admit that he may not have all the facts. Further, he must be willing to concentrate. The following pages were written for such a person.

Therefore, the most honest introduction I can offer the reader is a warning that, except for the use of numbers on the face of a clock to indicate rod positions (Fig. 1), the following material will not be a repetition of things you have heard or read previously about fly casting, for the ideas presented here were developed in spite of, rather than because of, accepted procedures.

I expect my role as a nonconformist will bring the wrath of a horde of experts down about my ample ears. But since my ears are old campaigners in what a guide associate once referred to as "The War of Hooks," I doubt that a little verbal discord will make them retract very much.

"Experts" (as a nomenclature) may occur in two varieties—genuine and synthetic. The genuine expert casts the fly for the sheer joy of accomplishment. Past, present, and future champions of the world are among their ranks. Their interest exceeds necessity, for some of them rarely fish. They are involved in a form of scientific research, and they may even agree with me that a "ceiling" in fly casting doesn't exist yet.

In contrast, there are the "synthetics." Most of these have fished for several years with success from their own viewpoint, for, if you have caught some fish and won a few bets from your friends, it's easy to become complacent. Most of them have a "pet" outfit that you should "buy one just like" because it has "lots of power." Most of them have spent season after season using ten feet more line than they can handle adequately. Most of them break the points off their flies on the back cast, and get innumerable tangles accompanied by innumerable epithets on a windy day, and most of them set flies off in the largest fish they induce to rise by setting the hook too hard. And most of them pounce with glee upon every novice they know, showering him with "dos" and "don'ts"; finally finishing with the famous old standby of snatching the rod and voicing the famous old quote of "watch me— here's exactly the way to do it."

You might think the two types of expert have little in common, but from a novice viewpoint there is one glaring similarity. Regardless of how sincere their intentions may be, neither casts the way he instructs others to do it. Still, I must emphasize that I have never known an expert who didn't begin as a novice.

During the past forty years I have read innumerable articles on casting the fly. I have attended lectures of every casting celebrity who appeared in my local Oregon area, and I have attended classes, at least one of which was conducted by a newly-crowned distance champion of the world.

Yet I have never met an expert of either type whose instruction coincided with, or even faintly resembled, his own casting technique.

I have seen a nationally known authority demonstrate a long cast with his arm extended full length overhead, and with the rod sweeping from nine o'clock in front to three o'clock behind. Not thirty seconds later he was telling members of his class to confine the stroke between "ten and one" and "above all, hold your elbows tightly to your sides."

A lot of water has passed under the bridge (and in my case, "under the boat") since that day, but the paradox was one I determined some day to solve. During the ensuing years as a fly tier, rod maker, casting instructor, and river guide, I think I have uncovered some of the factors that may help explain the almost universally misunderstood sport of fly casting, and I offer the following pages in response to what I consider to be a genuine need.

PROBLEMS

Two problems have caused an abundance of misunderstanding between instructors and their pupils in the past. The first involves the optical illusion that occurs when a spectator watches a genuine expert cast. One can actually see that the rod travels in a constant sweep, from horizontal in front to horizontal in back; one can see the use of the entire wrist, arm, and shoulder, and the caster may even step forward and back with the cast. After watching, one is convinced, despite what the caster says, that he is "fighting" his tackle; his rod merely acting as an extension of his arm.

So, taking rod in hand, you apply twice the usual force, and the fly goes five feet farther than usual. Then you apply ten times the effort, expecting the fly to go fifty feet farther. It won't.

The second problem evolves from the individuality of the expert himself. Concise information has been so skimpy that most of the really great casters have developed their own styles, indicating a high degree of inherent co-ordination, but sometimes developed to fit personal muscular peculiarities. Unhappily, such persons rarely have the knack of transferring their knowledge to others. Like the Jim Thorpes and Babe Ruths, their skills cannot be analyzed by a layman by merely watching. And, they, in turn, cannot understand why others cannot duplicate their feats.

So, my own childhood of almost spastic awkwardness may have been a sort of left-handed blessing. Each physical accomplishment required such concentration that the methods are etched in my memory. I tried for a full ten years before casting a fly more than forty feet. I have had pupils do it within the first hour. Be of good cheer if your first attempts have been unfortunate. Corrections are easy, and since I am convinced that misunderstanding is the root of all fly casting evils, I predict that the following material will be of help. I will even go so far as to predict that if existing records are broken it will be by methods described in these pages. I realize that few of my readers will aspire to become tournament competitors, most persons being contented with a top job of actual fishing. But in either event, the tools to work with will be presented here. Your proficiency will depend on your interest, coordination, improvisation, amount of practice, and choice of equipment.

I read recently that an ancient cathedral in Holland bears the inscription: "If it is true, it cannot be otherwise." Following this line of thought, fly casting has certain procedures that must be performed in a definite sequence for a definite reason. These are the only ways in which a fly outfit can be cast; it cannot be done otherwise. I will attempt to cover them, one by one, in proper sequence, as simply and thoroughly as possible.

The following pages are divided into several categories. Some are quite technical, requiring a mind ready for concentration. Some require the actual use of equipment, so that you enact each succeeding phase (and master it) before trying the next. Some are designed to stimulate an awareness of the outdoors, the water, the weather, and the myriad of living things about us. Many readers will scan such pages in a relaxed manner, but I predict that if a problem arises they will return to the technical portions, seeking an answer. I hope (and I am rather confident) that they will find it.

Though fly fishing may be centuries old, it started a lusty second childhood with the development of salt-water-proof lines, leaders, rods, and reels, opening uncounted thousands of miles of fishing frontier, and offering innumerable new species of fish, any of which will be more fun to take with a fly than by any other method. Yet this brings to mind a sobering thought.

With proper study and sufficient practice, there probably will be times when the fish are at your mercy, for under certain circumstances an artificial fly is more deadly than any other existing lure, including live bait. The feeling of mastery, of outwitting wild creatures in their own element, is probably the ultimate thrill and accomplishment of any sportsman.

But if you have such mastery, the creatures in turn are defenseless. The thrill lies in knowledge of mastery, not in wanton slaughter. Legal limits are designed to protect the interest of everyone, including the fish, just like the count of ten in boxing. A fisherman who would take more than the limit, or more than he needs, simply because he has the fish at his mercy, is in the same class with the champion fighter who would trample an opponent who has been counted out.

Let the fly rod be a beautiful and precise piece of recreational equipment—not a means of extermination. Remember this whenever you are given the "Indian sign."

I.

THE THEORY

FORTY YEARS of experience and observation have convinced me that the worst thing that can happen to a novice caster is to try to use a rod without knowing what he is trying to accomplish. Besides, it is harder to forget bad casting habits than to learn good ones.

I am certain· enough of this to state it as a rule, or "near rule." It is the only one I will venture as my own. Not that there aren't many other rules, and your eventual casting success will depend entirely upon your individual ability to follow those rules. They are not my rules, however, but rules of nature, which have been in existence for countless ages. I can only help interpret them for you.

One is the rule of gravity which causes a bullet fired horizontally, and a bullet dropped vertically from the same height, to strike the earth simultaneously. This means that regardless of the distance man may eventually cast a fly, he will have to do it in approximately the same length of time that it would take his line to drop vertically from the height of his rod tip. His only hope of escape would be a line that would plane slightly (which usually hampers it from turning over properly) , a hollow line filled with hydrogen or helium (which probably would be barred from competition, and would drift badly in the wind) or improvisations involving line tensions and inertia that hold the line up in the middle by pulling on both ends during the cast. The latter has been, and is being, done, partly by line design, and partly by manipulation, on every really long cast. This rule of gravity forces us to recognize the importance of timing and velocity in casting.

RESISTANCE

Another rule involves the viscosity of air, which offers resistance to any moving object, causing it to slow progressively as soon as its means of propulsion has ceased. Among "plug" casters, failure to abide by this rule results in the phenomenon of the "backlash," sometimes referred to in other terms not recorded here because of the flammability of paper.

In fly casting, viscosity merely limits your casting distance, demanding that you match your rod and line properly for top results. This rule is a nuisance that will affect every cast you ever make, except perhaps on the moon, where there is no atmosphere and gravity is only a fraction as troublesome, but inertia remains the same. I wonder if the first explorers have considered the possibility of a casting rod and suitable weights (perhaps just plastic bags filled with pebbles or sand) to test possible areas of "dry quicksand" ahead?

Next for consideration is inertia, the property of any object with weight to resist being moved. Let's consider a five-pound weight which can be pulled easily along a horizontal surface by a string of ten-pound strength, but which will break the string if jerked abruptly. This is the rule that forces changes in casting technique with each variation in weight of line or lure and in the force applied to the rod stroke, but which can also be of great value if interpreted and used properly.

Closely allied to the above rule is the one involving inertia of motion, frequently miscalled momentum, which causes a moving object to try to continue in the direction it was traveling. If, instead of pulling the weight, we shove it away abruptly, the string will break when it comes taut, but in this instance the motion of the weight caused the break, rather than our immediate effort. The effect of a given mass, masquerading as a heavier or lighter one, can help or hinder us, depending on our ability to diagnose its use properly.

Casting Principles: Levers

Now that we have taken a look at outside influences, let's study what happens to the rod itself in casting. Even the simplest cast involves a complexity of principles. I will try to spread them out for your inspection, like a deck of cards. However, in casting they must be performed almost simultaneously. First consideration should be levers.

The use of the simple lever could have started back with the Neanderthal man, who may have discovered he could pry a large boulder from over a rabbit burrow by placing one end of a small log under the boulder, with another rock crosswise under the log for a fulcrum; then by pushing down on the opposite end of the log he developed leverage. We have no record of the number of times he used this method to his advantage before the handle slipped and hit him in the nose. We do, however, have evidence of the incident from artists' sketches, invariably showing Neanderthal man with a flat nose.

The eventual use of various types of catapults (in barbaric warfare) indicated Man had learned that a lever, when released, will exert in reverse the amount of energy that has been applied. The application of slight force and great speed at the long end of a lever develops great force and slight speed at the short end. And by the same token, great force and slight speed on the short end will develop great speed but slight force at the long end. Thus, by using a long, light lever and applying force very near one end, we can attain speeds, on the other end, sufficient to throw small light objects farther than we could throw them by any other means.

This is one of the principles enabling us to cast, and defines the primary problem of all fishermen—that of sending a lighter lure over ever-increasing distances. Incidentally, it is the only principle easy to detect when watching another caster perform.

WHEEL ROTATION

But there are other principles to be considered in attaining still greater speeds. To best illustrate them, let's take several levers and use them for spokes in a wheel. Here the levers retain identical characteristics, for slight force and lots of speed applied to the rim of a wheel produces slight speed and lots of force near the hub. In reverse, lots of force applied near the hub produces great speed at the rim, and the speed will be greater if we apply more force, still nearer the center.

For purposes of absolute maximum speed, let us assume that we are grasping a spoke, or two spokes, connected at the axis, that extend completely across an imaginary rim. Our grasp is exactly in the middle so that two fingers are above and two below the axle or pivot point. We are able to rotate the wheel forward and backward for perhaps a fourth of its circumference by simply moving the top two fingers in one direction while the bottom pair move in the opposite way. We let our wrist rotate only when our fingers have moved far enough to threaten

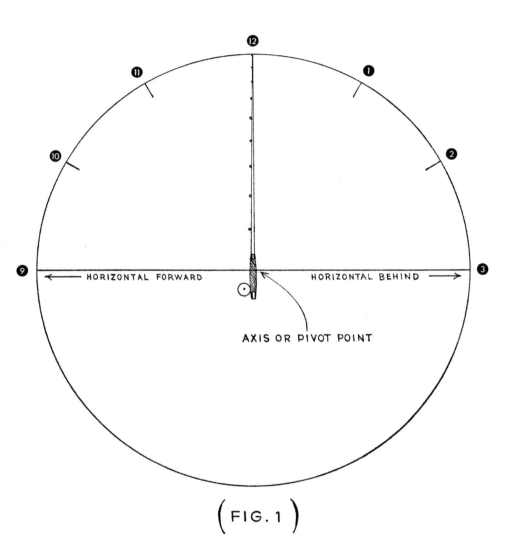

HORIZONTAL FORWARD

HORIZONTAL BEHIND

AXIS OR PIVOT POINT

(FIG. 1)

the firmness of our grip, at which point, if we reverse the rotation, the wheel will turn backward just as easily as it previously turned forward. No movement of our forearm, elbow, or upper arm is necessary. If we try to use them, the wheel usually will "wobble," and get out of control, instead of turning smoothly.

A little experimenting will show that we can keep the wheel moving, without wobble, back and forth in several positions: on our right side, in front, on our left side, (opposite) or even horizontally, overhead. The position of the wheel makes little difference. The important thing is being able to rotate it smoothly so that the wheel does not wobble. The significance of this should be emphasized, for a fishing rod, substituted for a spoke in a wheel (Fig. 2), will perform best if used identically. We will return to this comparison many times in the following pages.

It is timely to mention that the principle of plug casting should be understood before one attempts to cope with a fly rod. Although their use is similar in most respects, the fly rod requires additional analysis. First, a few illustrations will explain the casting rod, which propels a given amount of weight, namely the lure or sinker.

We have found that by holding a long, light lever by one end and applying force, we gain speed at the other end. Transplanting the lever into a wheel with an imaginary rim does not change its characteristics. Next, let's tie a weight to a piece of string threaded through an eyelet at the end of the spoke (lever), and pull the string until the weight is snug against the eyelet. Hold it taut at the wheel hub with the index finger.

As we rotate the wheel, we can feel the weight pulling on the string, and it pulls harder with greater speed of rotation. If suddenly we release the string, the weight will be thrown from the wheel with considerable velocity, though subsequent trials will show that we do not have adequate control over the direction it travels when released. If we try the same procedure using a lighter weight, it doesn't go as far, for a larger object, of a given material, will maintain its "momentum" longer when thrown at identical speeds.

THE FLAT SPOT—COAM

Searching for additional methods of speeding our light weight, let's try substituting a flexible spoke for the stiff one. Now we find that the inertia of the weight causes the tip of the spoke to lag behind when rotation is first begun, because the spoke bends. But when it straightens, and does catch up, the tip is traveling much faster than the tips of the other spokes, even though identical force was applied at the axis. It is going so fast that if we release the lighter weight at the instant the spoke straightens, it may go even farther than the heavier one did previously.

It is hard to believe that all this "pep" was developed by the spring of the straightening spoke, added to wheel rotation. As another source of speed, we discover that the weight, pulled snugly against the tip, did not follow the rim of the imaginary wheel this time. Instead, it took a short-cut, making a sort of "flat spot" on the rim of the wheel. This was caused by the fact that as the spoke bent, it shortened, and lagged behind the other spokes, catching up twice as fast later. Thus, the delay gave us more time to estimate the correct point of release by giving us a larger portion of the stroke in which to estimate corrections, improving our aim, and the "flat spot" gives us something to "sight" with. But the additional speed, which suddenly appeared from "nowhere," must also be explained.

An ordinary spool will serve the purpose of experimentation. Let's tie a weight to the end of a piece of string, and thread the string through the spool. Next hold the spool in your right hand and the back end of the string in your left hand so that the weight hangs a couple of feet below the spool. Swing the weight around and around the spool in a circle until it is going at an even speed. Then, abruptly pull some line in through the spool with your left hand. You may be surprised at the speed the weight suddenly gains, and as the radius of string is shortened the weight will pull as though it weighs considerably more.

The principle involved in this phenomenon has been given some such scientific name as the "conservation of angular momentum" (Fig. 2) , and I have been told that it even applies to orbits of planets and their satellites. But it is also evident in more common things, such as playground swings, cracking bullwhips, the sling that slew Goliath, and the spider watched by Robert Bruce.

It also affects our casting every time the rod bends enough to cause the tip to make a flat spot on the rim of the wheel. To conserve space I will refer to it as "COAM."

Before summarizing these various phases of casting, there is one more principle to be added to the repertoire of tricks for building speed. It is simply that while all other phases are occurring within the rotating wheel, we can move the entire wheel. If a point at the top of the wheel is traveling horizontally from east to west, its speed in relation to the earth and atmosphere can be increased by pushing the entire wheel, grasped by its axis, horizontally from east to west as it is rotated. If done simultaneously with the other forces, the flat spot can be extended, gaining more velocity for our cast. These are

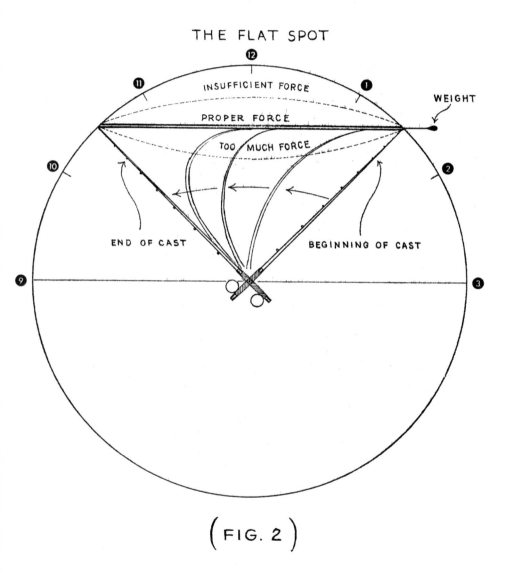

(FIG. 2)

the things you saw the champion caster do, and which you may have misinterpreted.

In summary, we have found that speed can be applied to a light weight by "rotating the wheel," by pushing or pulling the axis, by the force of our bent spoke straightening, and by the effect of COAM. The ultimate in casting will depend upon individual ability to blend them efficiently into a single unified force.

FLY *vs.* PLUG CASTING

There are three major differences of manipulation between fly rods and casting or spinning rods. Basically they are: differences in trajectory, timing, and inertia. The difference of trajectory in fly casting is so nearly self-compensating, because COAM supports it, that I will ignore it except to point out that a weight can be cast a hundred feet straight up, but a fly cannot. The importance of inertia and timing, however (inseparable twins), deserve high priority ratings.

The most important puzzle confronted in the inertia problem is that with a fly outfit there is no predetermined amount of weight to push against to form the all-important flat spot at the top of the imaginary wheel. In fact, there are seldom two consecutive casts with a fly rod that require identical manipulation. Although this may sound disheartening, "despair not." There is a little-known fact that equalizes things.

Simply that neither you nor the world's best fly casters know exactly what is going to happen when a series of fly casts is begun. The first cast is ALWAYS an experiment, the second is ALWAYS a correction, and the final cast is ALWAYS a further correction. There are no exceptions!

Constant practice with a single outfit can help us to

anticipate what usually will happen, but the real secret is in our ability to observe and correct. These corrections follow a pattern that I'll attempt to analyze.

DIFFERENCE IN INERTIA

Let's start by establishing the differences between the inertia of a fly line and the inertia of a casting weight. The casting weight, being constant, resists motion enough to bend the rod, helping us to build the all-important flat spot at the top of the wheel. The fly line, however, appears to have no such property, for no amount of weight or resistance is noticed when one pulls on the end of a loosely coiled fly line. But if we climb a tall ladder and dangle our line full length, straight down, we can feel its entire weight (Fig. 3). If we descend until half of the line is coiled on the ground, the line is only half as heavy, indicating that the only part furnishing weight is the portion hanging straight down.

If we take the "vertical" demonstration drawn above, and turn it on its side, the characteristics remain identical, except that the line furnishes "inertia" instead of "weight," and the straightness and position of the line are temporary, rather than permanent (Fig. 4). Thus it becomes imperative that, to cast a fly line, we must establish at least temporary inertia to push against, which can only be furnished by a portion of straight line following the rod tip horizontally before and during each cast, and any portion not following will not aid, and may even hamper inertia. The "flat spot" must be built into every cast, regardless of the amount of inertia available, but once built, it must be used immediately or it will virtually disappear into thin air.

Such maneuvering requires some preliminary motion before the force is applied to the cast, and this is one of

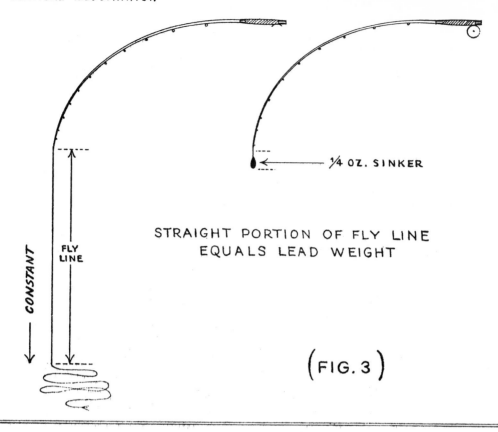

¼ OZ. SINKER

STRAIGHT PORTION OF FLY LINE
EQUALS LEAD WEIGHT

FLY
LINE

CONSTANT

(FIG. 3)

VARIABLE...DEPENDING UPON FORCE EXERTED

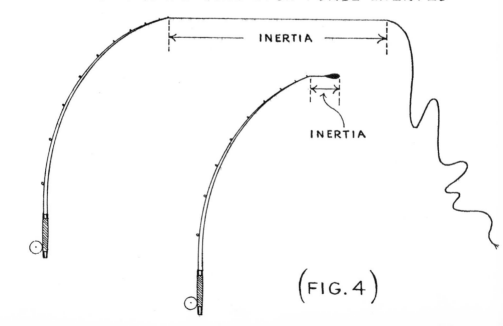

INERTIA

INERTIA

(FIG. 4)

the things likely mistaken for part of the "power stroke" when watching a distance expert perform. The success of any fly caster's performance depends on *how many feet of straight line* he can coax into *following his rod tip* before he applies maximum force to the cast. Whenever your casts don't work, I recommend you read this paragraph once more, for it applies to every cast you will ever make with a fly rod.

Again the Flat Spot

It's timely here to review the flat spot and to further investigate its functions. We have seen that balanced amounts of flexibility, inertia, and applied force will cause the rod tip to cut across the top of a circle in a precisely straight line. An increase in any one or a combination of the three will cause the flat spot to become concave or dip down in the middle. This causes the weight to catch up with, and try to pass, the tip prematurely, when force is relaxed, because of an overdose of inertia at the start, and an overdose of COAM afterward. Thus, the rod tip attempts to straighten in midstroke, gaining elevation and loitering directly in the path of the pursuing line. On the other hand added stiffness of the rod or a decrease in inertia or force results in convexity of the flat, losing the advantages of COAM and resiliency that we might have utilized, because, in this instance, the following line isn't straight any more.

Adjustments

Significant here is the possibility of having too much of any one of the factors and of compensating with a lesser portion of either or both of the others. Thus, to correct for a stiffer rod (convexity), use more inertia (more straight line), a quicker stroke, or both. Too heavy a weight (concavity) indicates less flexibility (a stiffer rod) or less speed, or both. Too light a weight (convexity) indicates more flexibility (a more flexible rod) or more speed, or both. Try to arrange more straight line before the cast.

In the case of the fly line, where inertia is always an unknown quantity, one needs to be alert in estimating corrections. Luckily, there are well defined visible indications as to the amount and variety of correction.

Of some importance here is recognition of the fact that whereas the casting weight has a tendency to continue in a straight line, the fly line has no such characteristic, but will follow blindly and blandly wherever the rod tips leads as long as the tip continues to accelerate. Thus, a perfectly executed cast can be ruined by continuing to increase force beyond the end of the available flat spot, causing it to become unnecessarily convex. Here the tip leaves its horizontal path and starts downward, whereupon the entire line, following the tip, also will leave its original course and slant down. This revolting development recompenses us if we remember that acceleration beyond the flat spot will cause our line to slant downward (convexity), indicating the needed correction —a shorter stroke or more force in subsequent casts.

KILLING THE CAST

Before we go farther into errors and their corrections, we must establish some reference points for various phases of the cast. The first occurrence requiring a label is the zone in which the speed of the line first equals and begins to exceed the speed of the rod tip. This must occur just before the tip goes over the end of the flat spot, to avoid pulling the line down. This is referred to as killing the cast (Fig. 5). In all cases, it means the zone of the

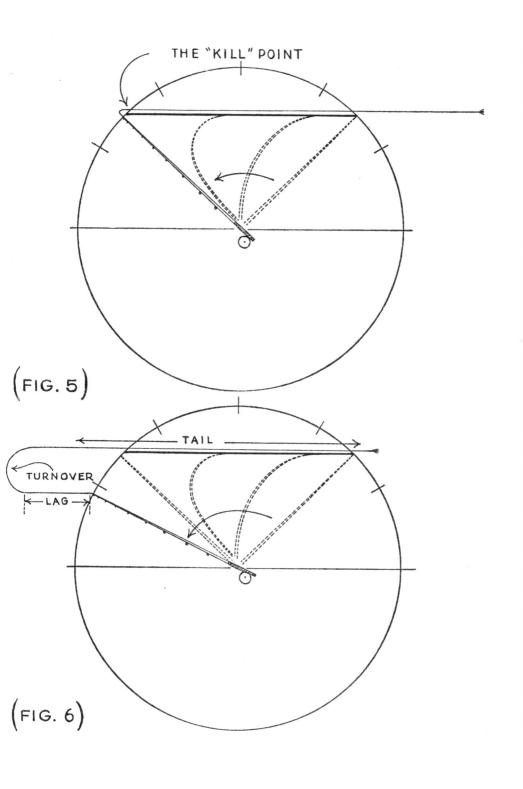

THE "KILL" POINT

(FIG. 5)

TURNOVER
LAG
TAIL

(FIG. 6)

rod stroke beyond which the constructive portion of the cast is finished and there is little if any directional control.

LAG, TURNOVER, TAIL

After a fly cast has been killed, the straight portion of the line that has been following the rod tip through the flat begins to pass the tip and COAM is transferred from the rod to the line instead. Since the line must not be permitted to slide out of the guides during the power stroke, it can only pass beyond the tip by forming a letter "U" turned on its side (Fig. 6). In this, the lower segment remains static, but the upper segment continues to travel until it eventually turns over completely and is in a straight line again in the opposite direction. Since the static portion of the "U" is left behind, I will refer to it as the "lag." The moving segment, being the last portion to follow the applied force of the cast, will be referred to as the "tail," while the curved segment of the "U" which is constantly turning over, and leading the tail along, will simply be called the "turnover." This is the constantly moving point in the line where COAM continues to occur until the line has completely straightened. This should not be confused with the words "turn" and "over" which must be used occasionally to describe other phases of the cast.

CONCAVITY AND CONVEXITY—BUILDING "STRAIGHT LINE" INERTIA

We have established that acceleration beyond the flat spot causes the cast to slant downward, indicating that we should kill the cast earlier in the stroke. Now, let's consider what happens when we apply insufficient force, throughout the stroke, again causing the flat to become convex.

Obviously, the last half of the stroke again is slanted down by the rod tip that slants down, but this has been preceded by the first half of the stroke, which slanted up for the same reason. This conflict results in the tail slanting up as the lag slants down, for the cast was killed while the tail was pointed above the horizon. As one continues to climb, the other continues to drop, causing the turnover to form such a broad curve that COAM and velocity are lost due to air resistance, like a javelin being thrown sideways. Thus, the last portion of the tail falls in a heap rather than straightening out at the finish. Correction on the next cast should be greater acceleration across the flat to shorten the rod more at midstroke, assuring a later kill point. Control over the present cast ceased when the broadness of the turnover formed, so all corrections must be saved for the next cast as control has been lost on the present one.

Reversing the conditions, let's consider a flat made concave by applying too much force too early in the stroke. Again, due to earlier premature killing, which occurs whenever the rod begins to straighten, the causes described in the above illustration are nearly reversed. This in turn reverses the effects, so that the lag and turnover slant upward, as if a new cast had been started, while the tail, slanting downward, must cross the lag or rod at some point, usually resulting in a tangled line or leader. This is probably the most universal of all fly casting errors, and is caused by underestimating the amount of straight line inertia we have built. The almost instinctive tendency is to try to correct by using more force rather than less. This is like adding fuel to the fire, for more concavity will result.

If you have this difficulty, and have practiced incorrectly for several seasons, you may have trouble breaking the habit. Bear in mind that the maximum force AL-WAYS is applied in the *last* 10 percent of the stroke before the kill point—which merely defines the difference between constant acceleration and force applied promiscuously.

Changing to a size lighter line will help compensate for a tendency to fight the tackle by helping flatten the concavity of the rod in midstroke, but it is well to bear in mind that the rod should not *stop* at the kill point. Only the *acceleration* stops. Continued use of a degree of force will get the rod out of the line's path. This maneuver may have been misinterpreted when you watched the expert perform, because it looks like a portion of the power stroke.

SUMMARY OF CORRECTIONS

In summary, we have established several aids in correcting mistakes. If the cast slants downward, we have applied force beyond the flat. The correction is to kill the cast earlier.

If our cast doesn't turn over completely, the line was not as "heavy" as we thought. Proper correction is to use more speed across the flat.

If the cast swoops down upon us, threatening our ears, or tangling with the rod tip or "lag," our line was "heavier" than we thought. To correct, apply less force or make certain the most force is applied later, just before the kill point, or a combination of the two.

These corrections are tools to use in every cast. When they can be summoned quickly from memory, we are ready to begin practice with a rod.

II.

THE PRACTICE

PRELIMINARY TO PRACTICE, two safety factors should be observed. First it is advisable to wear glasses of some sort when fly fishing. If no visual correction is needed, sun glasses, preferably polaroids, in the lighter shades, will fill the bill. If correction is needed, wide vision sun glasses, ground to prescription, is something to write Santa about.

Second, I discourage the use of an actual hook in practice. A small tuft of fluorescent yarn tied to the end of the leader will do just as well. It offers about the same air resistance as a fly, will prevent the leader from "cracking the whip," is easy to see, and is economical. For practice, a leader four to five feet long, of eight or ten pound monofilament, is fine.

ASSEMBLING THE TACKLE

It is always important that the line comes off the reel in such a manner that it passes no corners between the spool and the stripping guide (the first large one on the butt section of the rod). Any other route will cause unnecessary wear. Also, it is important that the line pass through ALL of the guides on the rod. This does not include the little round ring just above the grip, as this is to hook the fly into when not in use. The only way of being certain you thread all the guides is to pull the end of the line to the side after threading. In my nearly 40 years of guiding fishermen, I would estimate that someone has failed to rig his rod and reel properly on at least 25 percent of the trips.

PRACTICE LOCATION

The practice locality should be one with water in front of the caster. It is almost impossible for the novice to start without water on which to practice the pickup and roll cast. Also, water will save much wear on the line. The water should be still rather than running. A pond or pool that can be worked from any direction is best. A swimming pool may qualify unless it is surrounded by a fence, which might damage your line or rod if your cast tangles with it.

Assuming the average reader is a novice, right-handed, and casting over water, let's continue, performing each phase in turn. Never skip to the next phase until the present one is thoroughly understood. Figure 7 represents a typical pond, with the * (star) representing the caster in various locations, with wind directions and coincident problems indicated by shaded areas. See figure 10 also.

The only major problem in fly casting that doesn't get easier with practice is simply that of getting enough line out through the tip to start casting. Like eating Chinese noodles, there is no graceful way of doing it. The method I present is the safest of several inadequate time-wasting ways, for it eliminates the hazard of a broken tip or the nuisance of possibly contaminating your reel and line with abrasive dust or sand. A right-handed person should approach the pond so that any breeze blows from his left. (Southpaws opposite.) This would be the east shore in figure 7. Pick a spot where the terrain behind

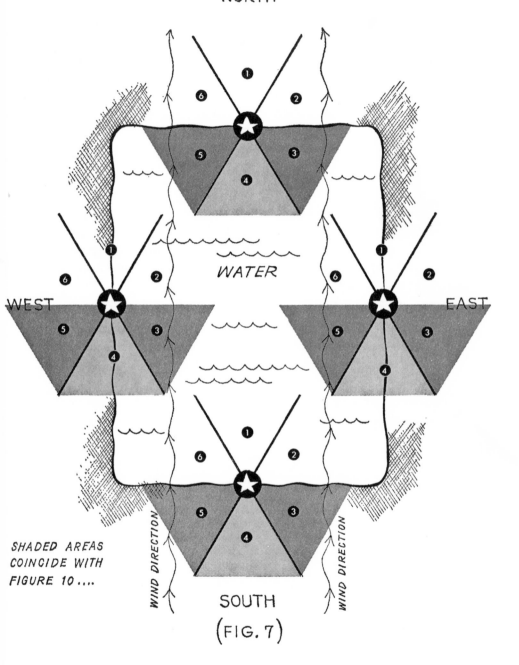

NORTH

6   1   2

5   3

4

WATER

WEST

6   1   2

5   3

4

6   1   2

5   3

4

EAST

6   1   2

5   3

4

SHADED AREAS
COINCIDE WITH
FIGURE 10 ....

WIND DIRECTION

WIND DIRECTION

SOUTH

(FIG. 7)

you is free of obstructions such as trees, bushes, tall weeds, or spectators. Stand as near the water level as possible without risking footing and balance. Drop the tuft of yarn, leader, and end of line into the water near the shore-line, being careful not to pull the knot, where the leader and line are joined, back through the tip guide. Gently pull about an arm's length of line from the reel, place the tip guide barely in the water and jerk with the tip, rather abruptly, away from shore. At this point, the loose line between the reel and first guide should have slid out through the tip. Without raising the rod, pull more line from the reel and jerk to the side again. Repeat as often as necessary. If your rod nears shore on the other side, reverse the direction of the jerks, so that force is applied away from the the shore to avoid possible tip damage.

The number of jerks necessary to get the "working" line out will vary with different outfits. Those using a tapered fly line will have more difficulty since they will be trying to get the fine line in the water to drag the coarse line, from near the reel, out through the guides. Holding the loose line between the reel and first guide, slightly above the rod, with the left hand may help to slide it out. If, in changing directions, the tip tends to tangle with line already in the water, take a half step backward before changing.

ROLL CAST

When you have 10 to 12 feet of line between the rod tip and the leader, you are ready to try the first roll cast.

Considered difficult by many fishermen, the roll cast is actually simple because it does not involve a backcast, and it requires little if any timing. It is the most consistent of all casts, for the amount of straight line following the rod tip will never exceed the distance from the *rod tip*

at 12 o'clock to the surface of the water straight below.
Give the stroke across the flat plenty of speed. This helps
pick up the tail, which is always in the water, and usually
in front of you, when a roll cast is started.

If the first roll fails to pick up the tail, and turn it
over, don't despair. Simply do the same thing time after
time until it does turn over. It will travel in whatever
direction the flat is pointed, regardless of where the line
may be when the cast is started, but enough force must
be used to cause the slack portion of the tail (which may
be twice as long) to follow the turnover.

But there is one thing to watch. Never aim a roll cast
that will cross any part of the slack tail of the line in the
water. If you do, the tail, which rises up from the water,
will tangle with the lag, which has crossed over it. The
cast must be aimed far enough to the right or left so that
the tail will miss the rest of the line as it rises up and
turns over.

Assuming that you have 15 or 20 feet of line and
leader in the water in front of you, let's try the first roll.
To prevent more line from feeding out, hold the line
snugly under the index finger of the rod hand. Begin the
roll by raising the rod tip waist high. Bring it *slowly*
around to the right, raising the tip gradually, until it is
not quite directly behind and about 2 o'clock height.
This does not mean your hand should be behind you, as it
should still be about 12 inches or so in front of your right
shoulder and quite stationary.

To complete the roll, bring the tip of the rod forward
to a vertical or 12 o'clock position. Bring it fast enough
so that the line does not have time to fall under the tip
as it moves, but not fast enough to cause the rod to bend
much. Continue the stroke past the vertical, without
pause, creating a flat spot with constantly increasing pow-

er to 10 o'clock, with a surge between 11 and 10. Some 60 percent of the force should be applied by gripping your hand, which has been relaxed and partially open. The gripping should be applied gradually, to coincide with the rod stroke.

Some 30 percent of the force should be applied by tilting your wrist, again timed to coincide with the rod. Don't move your arm. It should not furnish any power yet, and should remain relaxed, to hold merely the weight of the rod, except during the surge on the forward stroke. If you try to throw the entire rod, you don't have a rotating wheel any more.

RIGHT ROLL

When the forward stroke reaches 10 o'clock, kill the force by relaxing your hand slightly, drop the rod to 9 o'clock, and observe what has happened. This is a "right roll" because the rod was manipulated on your right side.

If the leader and fly rose from the water and moved farther out into the pond, everything is fine. If it picked up and came toward you, you have used too much force, or force too early. The theory of the roll is that the fly and leader remain anchored until the turnover has traveled beyond them (forward), whereupon they follow it. If they pick up before the turnover reaches them, the turnover had too much speed, a result of too much force, If, on the other hand, they didn't pick up at all, simply repeat the entire roll again, using more force until they do turn over. If they are sunk deep, each turnover that passes above will lift them closer to the surface until they eventually will pick up—important with fast-sinking lines. Thus, roll casting is easier with a well-dressed line and

floating fly than with sinking lines and flies. However, it
is a useful tool with either.

LEFT ROLL

Assuming that your first roll turned over properly,
let's proceed with the practice. Since the line is still too
short to cast well, let's repeat the process of stripping line
from the reel, yard by yard. Feed it out by holding the
tip low and jerking alternately left and right until there
is a total of three rod lengths of line out. The objective
this time is a point to the right of the sunken leader.

To get the rod pointed in the opposite direction from
the target, it must be brought to the left side at 3 o'clock,
slowly. Hold the right hand in front of the *left* shoulder
to prevent the rod from striking it. There are two ways
to accomplish this, one has a distinct advantage. The
first is to hold the rod at 2 o'clock on the left side, with
the right hand grasping the rod in front of the left shoulder, with the *palm of the hand toward the face.* This is a
true *backhand* cast position. As far as coordination is concerned, it requires exactly opposite timing from the roll
executed on the right side, because the forward stroke will
be a "pull." The change can be confusing to a novice.

The alternative, and the *best,* is to hold the right hand
in front of the left shoulder so that the *back of the hand* is
toward the face. In this position the timing remains
identical with the roll on the right side, because the forward stroke will be a "push." For this left side roll, it is
not necessary to hold the hand against the left shoulder
—merely in front of it, in a comfortable position.

To continue practice, bring the rod at waist height
slowly around on the left side, making certain that the
back of the right hand remains toward your face. Execute
the roll and correct as described previously. This is the

"left roll" because the line and rod are manipulated on the left side. Remember that the force should be applied more by "rocking" the grip in the hand than by using the wrist and arm. Thus, the right hand should still be in the same position in front of the left shoulder when the cast ends.

The cast should work well at this distance for there is time to watch the turnover. Also, the tail remains anchored better, permitting less critical timing as well as better indications of correction. But feed more line until the next roll will be of 30-35 feet, a good practice distance for most outfits. Remember to relax your hand except when force is being applied.

Having completed one short right roll and one longer left roll, let's do another right roll aimed at a point to the left of the fly, then a left roll aimed at a point to the right of the fly. Alternate repeatedly until it becomes automatic and can be done by feel alone—with eyes closed.

Compensating for Breeze

Next, let's do a series of right rolls, each aimed a little to the left of the last one, until the final one lands within less than a rod length of the shoreline to your left. This is the direction the wind is coming from. If it is blowing strongly, you may have trouble getting the last few rolls to turn over against it.

Added force doesn't seem to help much for the fly and leader seem to rise too high, getting caught in the wind. The result is that they blow back toward the caster. This is caused by the wind pressing against the rod and dragging on the line, causing some resistance and friction. The rod bends more than usual now with the same amount of force.

Therefore, 12 o'clock is no longer where it was previously, and though you are pushing from 12 to 10 o'clock on the grip, the tip is applying force from 1 to 11 o'clock because of rod curvature. This projects the cast higher than it should go. To correct, apply force beyond 10 o'clock, or even down to 9 o'clock if the wind blows very strong, till the flat spot becomes level again. This actually permits the use of more force by delaying the kill point, as if the line weight were greater than usual. Remember, this is used only AGAINST wind. If the wind is too strong, Area No. 4 (Figures 7 and 10) becomes impractical.

Reversing the procedure, let's try a succession of left rolls, each aimed a little to the right of the preceding one, until the last one rests 10 feet from the shoreline at the right. Now the wind comes from behind, causing little or no difficulty in getting the turnover to force the tail to follow. In fact, there is an advantage to be gained from the wind—an advantage we have seen in sailboats, kites, hoops, etc.

In the case of all those, the force exerted by the wind is in fairly direct proportion with the area it has to blow against. Wind effect is more noticeable on a tall sail than on a short one, and more noticeable on a high rolling hoop than on a low one. Since the turnover of the roll cast can be compared to a rolling hoop, we should make the roll loop larger to take advantage of help from the wind.

So we must aim the cast higher, increasing the distance between the top of the turnover and the water, so that the loop is taller. The broadened turnover does "catch" more wind, turning over with less applied force on the rod grip.

For proof, point the roll cast at right angles with the wind (Fig. 7, Areas 5 or 6), then feed out line little by little until it will no longer roll over. This seems to establish a temporary limit in distance for the tackle. But trying the same amount of line with the wind blowing from your back, it turns over easily (Fig. 7, Area 1).

When a strong wind helps, it is possible to roll cast 20 to 30 feet farther than the same outfit will roll cast in calm weather. Under conditions of wind, the roll cast is the best of all casts, for the roughened surface of the water cancels the extra disturbance of the roll, which normally would startle the fish. Another advantage in the roll cast is that one can avoid throwing knots in the leader, an item that occurs frequently when a standard false cast heads directly into the wind. Another wind bonus is that all kinds of insects are likely to be blown from the shore into the water by the wind.

A Mental Hazard

I have seen strong men (one of whom was a nationally known casting instructor) cuss and gnash their teeth all day because of a 10-15 mile-per-hour breeze. I also have seen frail women catch beautiful limits during gusts from 40-50 miles per hour (Fig. 10), all the while blessing the wind that permitted them to reach fish with a roll cast that had always "spooked" the fish before, even from their longest casts. This indicates than many of the so-called "casting hazards" are mental.

Roll Cast Summary

In summary of the roll casting session, let's enumerate the things we have learned. First, no matter how deep the fly has sunk, it can be brought to the surface, ready to recast, by a succession of rolls. This also means that it never will be necessary to shorten the line to less than 30 or 35 feet to recast. This is a real time-saver in eliminating the clumsy feeding-out procedure.

Second, a roll will travel in the direction you apply force.

Third, a roll on the right side is a right roll although it is aimed to the left of the fly, and vice versa. To move the fly straight ahead, use alternating rolls, right and left. It is important NOT to aim a right roll to the right of the fly or left roll to the left of it, for in these instances the fly may pick up and come directly toward your face.

Fourth, make the cast low and hard AGAINST the wind, being certain the maximum force is later in the stroke than usual. Make the cast high and "soft" with the wind, being certain to kill the cast earlier in the stroke than usual.

The last few points might be handy to have on a card during practice sessions.

In addition to the above, we have learned that the wind is not a thing to be dreaded, but rather something that can help if we work with it and understand its influence.

Before advancing into the realm of the false cast, there is one more roll-casting exercise that we should practice. While facing straight across the pond with the breeze coming from our left, let's assume we are facing west. This would indicate that the breeze is southerly as the shoreline to the left would be the south; the shoreline to the right—north. Starting with a right roll toward the west, continue with a series of right rolls until you are rolling south. Count the number as you roll. In most cases, there will be six or more. Using a series of left rolls, work back toward west, using fewer casts with larger gaps between. Continue on to north, then switch to right rolls and work back to the south, again using fewer casts

with larger gaps between. This demonstrates more forc-
ibly that wherever you send the turnover, the tail will follow. Continue practice until you can take the fly from
north to south or the reverse in about four rolls. If this
isn't working properly, you may be forgetting the importance of holding the rod in the *opposite direction* from
the target. In theory, you may be wobbling the rim of the
imaginary wheel in which the rod is the spoke. Or you
may not be waiting long enough with the rod behind you
for the line to hang *straight below the tip.*

THE CROSS CAST

The next maneuver I refer to as the cross cast because
it travels from one point of the compass to the direct opposite. The line and fly should be well dressed so that
they float on the surface. Then, to avoid unfavorable
wind, move to the south end of the pond, where the wind
will come from behind (south) as one faces the water.

Let's assume that you have fed out line and rolled to
the east, to your right, with the rod, line, and leader still
pointing east. Without moving them, turn slowly until
you face west (left). Starting with the rod at 2 o'clock
and pointed slightly north of east, proceed to cast just as
if the line and fly were being rolled. Keep the rod tip
slightly north of 12 o'clock as it passes overhead and end
the cast with the tip still pointed slightly north of west,
or in theory the top of the wheel must be tilted so that the
top rim is north of its axis. This helps the tail of the cast
to pass on your right side (north) instead of popping you
in the back of the neck if it hasn't lifted properly from
the water.

Rod, line, and fly should now be pointed west. Corrections are the same as usual for the flat and for wind, but
the possibility of the line being sunken and "anchored"

now enters the picture. Since the cross cast uses a genuine pickup rather than a roll, anchoring can affect you. A roll cast can be repeated over and over, but the cross cast pickup must be done correctly the first time—just like a parachute jump. If only a few feet of the end of the line are sunk, the cross cast may still go where it is aimed, but it will either seem sodden and sluggish throughout the power stroke or will burst from the water in midstroke, killing the cast prematurely and frequently tangling from the resulting concavity of the flat. If the line is anchored too substantially to pick up properly, you must turn again and start all over with a roll cast to the east. Follow immediately with the cross cast before the line has a chance to sink deep enough to anchor again.

TIMING THE PICKUP

The ideal time to apply power to the pickup would be just as the anchor releases, when the line is no longer gripped by the friction of the water. At that moment the line is straightest, having been pulled taut by the water. Since it has not been free long enough to sag, it will be quite straight, and the entire length will follow across the flat with a minimum of effort. Thus, the timing on a pickup appears quite critical.

How are we going to tell the proper time to apply power? Simply by turning the head and watching. When the knot joining the line and leader comes to the surface, we know the line is no longer anchored, for the fly and leader never anchor very much. If the rod has not passed 12 o'clock, we can make the cross cast. If it has passed 12 o'clock, we simply roll the line back to the east beyond where it came from, and cross cast on the next pickup instead. Remember the most power is still applied LATE

in the stroke, and the straighter the line, the more gradual its application should be.

Let's digress for a moment to the subject of head
turning. For some obscure reason "casting sages through
the ages" have condemned to utter degradation any fly
caster who turns his head to observe what his line does
while it is behind him. They consider the act a confes-
sion of inadequacy, if not actual cowardice, like looking
behind you at night in a cemetery.

As a result, they have wedged apart two identical acts.
They put the "halves" in separate categories: the forward
cast and the backward cast, proclaiming them to be entirely different from each other; that one is always in full
view, while the other remains forever hidden, and there
are almost as many explanations for these differences as
there are expert casters.

I don't doubt that there are casters who could fish
our western streams all day without looking behind them.
There are also people who can snap their fingers and
make an elephant disappear, but you and I are not likely
to duplicate either feat. To us, a forward cast and a backcast will remain identical except for direction and wind.
It makes no difference to the rod—why us?

Twice I have had the "privilege" of boating rabid
members of the "fraternity of the forward look." As I
recall, one of them left 11 flies in trees, while the other
deposited 13 flies during their respective days of fishing.
At the end of the trips, neither expressed much apprecia-
tion for the beautiful foliage along the McKenzie River,
as viewed from a boat.

If man was not intended to turn his head to look behind him, he would have been created with eyes on the
sides of his head like a duck or a rabbit, so when in doubt,
turn and look. And don't let anyone talk you out of it.

Returning to the cross cast, let's assume that you have completed a right cross cast and the line and rod are now pointing west. Without moving them, turn to the right until you face east and do a left cross cast from the west to the east so that the line again passes to the north. Turn your head and watch the pickup, making certain it is straight and on the surface before applying force. Alternate these cross casts until they become thoroughly familiar and you can time them with your eyes closed. Now you are ready for your first backhand cast.

BACKHAND CASTING

Let's assume that you have completed a cross cast toward the west and that the rod and line are pointing west. You face slightly northwest so that by turning your head, you can look east easily. Begin a cross cast with the rod west at 9 o'clock. Raise it with increasing speed to 12 o'clock, watching all the while for the leader knot or drop fly to come to the surface. If it does, continue without pausing to 1 o'clock north, keeping the palm toward the face and ending with abrupt force just before the kill. Then relax your hand and let the rod down to 3 o'clock behind while watching the line turn over. This is the first backhand cast in which the power has been applied with a pull instead of a push on the rod grip. Although the action of the rod and line are identical with what you have done previously, the "feel" of the cast may be entirely alien. This is the one that tempts people to use their biceps on the pickup rather than their hand and wrist. Holding elbows tightly against the sides is no preventive for it still permits arm swinging at the elbow, but holding your hand farther to the side may help.

Or there may be a tendency to grip the rod too tightly, resulting in a "bounce back" which tangles the line when the cast is killed. Wobbling the wheel so that the path of the rod curves is another common pitfall. By turning the head to observe, one can correct all these errors.

MORE BACKCASTING

Practice the backhand diligently, for it is a very important factor in long-distance casting. When it is working well, concentrate on ending the cast well above the water (earlier kill) and delay dropping the rod until the cast has turned over, so that the fly, rod tip, and lag drop simultaneously from the same height.

If the lag touches the water first, correct it with more speed before the kill. If this causes a tangle, kill the cast less abruptly so the rod gets out of the tail path faster. Observe closely how much time is required for the line to turn over. Practice this until it works smoothly.

Then, try the backhand as usual, but instead of dropping the tip toward the east, start raising it slowly toward 12 o'clock as soon as the fly has passed you. This should be timed so that the tip is approaching 12 o'clock and traveling west while the fly and leader are still turning over traveling east. This timing of opposing forces furnishes the lag with enough pull at both ends to keep the middle from sagging. This in turn gives the caster a straighter line to push against. If overdone, the effect of COAM will snap the fly off. Used moderately it anchors the line enough in midair to pull out the sag.

Continue the cast forward toward the west, as usual. The only new factor to be considered is that the line must be slightly lower than the rod tip (behind) when maximum power is applied, to furnish trajectory. On the second stroke, if it is higher, there is only one direction the tip can pull it—downward. However, the tip can lift, somewhat, on line that is below it. The amount of lift contributes in establishing the trajectory of the cast, and, although essential, this is of little value when compared to plug casting.

You have now completed your first genuine backcast.

Your west cross cast has become a forward cast simply because you are constantly facing west. Continue to practice the pickup and backcast, letting the forward cast rest on the water for a short time before each pickup. Practice until it is thoroughly familiar.

FALSE CASTING

Before going on to the next project, let's return to the first location. Feed and roll out the line until line and rod are pointed west. Now repeat the pickup, backcast, and forward cast as before. On the forward cast, if the line tends to drop on the water before the fly, shorten the stroke, applying power relatively late, but killing the cast early. Practice until the fly touches the water at the same time as the line, or even before. Continue to watch the backcast each time. When you have practiced until the backcast has become automatic, and the forward casts are turning over properly, you are ready to explore the field of false casting.

The false cast, contradictory to its title, is possibly the most genuine of all casts, and certainly the most useful. About 80 percent of the corrections of a skilled caster are made during a series of false casts. The term "false" has been used because you start the next cast before it has time to drop on its apparent target. Actually, the backcast you have been using, is a false cast, for you have been sending it forward, where it came from, before the fly has had time to drop to the ground behind. However, the term usually is used in reference to a series in which

neither the forward nor the backward casts are permitted
to touch.

Begin the false cast with the rod low and the line on
the water pointing west. Do a pickup and backcast in
the usual way so that the tail passes on your right. Start
the forward cast in the usual way, dropping the rod tip
slightly after the kill, but raising it again toward 12
o'clock as soon as the fly passes you, so that the tip arrives
at 12 o'clock on the backcast at about the same time the fly
turns over in front of you. This keeps the lag from
falling, and the better it is timed, the less forceful the
stroke will need to be. Complete the backcast (without pausing at 12 o'clock), then complete another forward cast (again without pausing). Continue these alternately so that the line remains constantly in the air,
without touching either the water in front or the ground
behind. Facing west, you are now performing a series
of right false casts. The left series will be covered later.

Your first reaction to a series of false casts probably
will be that things are happening pretty fast, perhaps
more rapidly than your thoughts and muscles can cope
with. And the shorter the line, the more critical the timing becomes. In an attempt to hurry, you are likely to
use more strength than necessary, sometimes resulting in
a longer stroke, which aims the cast downward, making
the timing more critical than ever. To correct, shorten
the stroke until the turnover actually climbs a little "uphill." This applies equally to the forward and backcasts.

Your line will have farther to fall now, giving you
more time to plan the next cast in the opposite direction.
If the line tangles on either the rod or the lag, remember
that the kill does *not* require the rod to *stop*. It merely
requires that the *speed be reduced,* after which it can continue to drop downward quickly, to avoid the tail, then

come back up again (after the fly passes) in preparation
for the opposite cast. Incidentally, this maneuver creates
the illusion referred to previously.

FEELING FOR THE WEIGHT

Continue the series indefinitely, for the adage about
necessity being the mother of invention holds true in
this instance, and it takes a tired hand and arm to find
easier ways of handling the rod. Besides there are some
points to be considered while false casting is in progress.

Concentrate on using as little effort as possible and
still keep the false cast from touching the ground or water in either direction. Grip the rod *only while force is
being applied,* and then only enough to prevent it from
turning in your grasp. Thirty-five feet can be false cast
with the average outfit by grasping the rod with a single
finger. Don't overestimate the power required, for a line
that is perfectly straight moves as a unit, and requires
little more force than an arrow of the same weight. When
the line is properly straight, the caster can feel its weight,
as if it were an inflexible object. Experienced casters feel
for the weight frequently, instead of looking behind. If
the weight is not there, when it should be, they will look
behind immediately. A variety of things can cause one
to lose the weight. Usually it is a gust of wind, not as yet
felt. It might be that the line touched a tree branch, hit
the horns of an approaching bull, or, even worse, struck
your spouse, whom you thought to be napping in the car.
A fly hook placed where an earring normally would be
worn can disrupt the most pleasant fishing expedition.

GRIPPING THE ROD

With your false casts still traveling back and forth in
the air, let's think next about methods of gripping the

rod plus the allied complications. So far we have been performing all maneuvers with the same length of line, which has been prevented from sliding out during casts by the pressure of a forefinger against the rod grip. Now we find it necessary to vary the length we are false casting. The simplest thing to do is to release the line from under the finger. First, strip some line from the reel so there are 15 to 20 feet of slack between the reel and the point the forefinger is holding against the cork grip. Then, as you begin to apply power to a stroke, suddenly release the line from under the finger.

If the line falls in a heap instead of going anywhere, don't be disappointed, for the experiment was intended to prove that a cast can be killed as effectively by a sudden release of line as any other way. But it can also be of use.

SHOOTING LINE

Pull the line in to the usual 35 feet and hold it under the forefinger, still leaving slack between the hand and reel. Then, pick it up and continue false casting. This time while false casting, pretend that a fish has risen a few feet beyond the distance your line will reach. Obviously more line must be fed to reach him, but this time let's wait until all the force has been applied to the forward stroke. Then release the line just as the rod reaches the kill point. Barring accidents, quite a bit of your line should have fed out through the rod guides. Shorten the line to the usual length, roll it, pick it up, and repeat the whole process many times, until your fly alights at about the same distance each time. If the line doesn't feed as well as it should, the line and rod guides may be rough or gummy with dressing. Or perhaps the line is being slowed by friction.   (Did you miss one of the guides while threading?)

On the contrary, if the line feeds too easily (as can occur in the use of torpedo lines), the fly may not turn over completely, an indication that the turnover has lost its COAM. Either more force should have been applied or the slack should have been held back a trifle. Any approach toward ways of accomplishing this brings us back to the subject of gripping the rod.

PROPER LINE HANDLING

When we release the line from under the finger of the right hand, we have lost complete control over it as far as that hand is concerned, for the right hand must remain the axis of the wheel, instead of searching for elusive line. Thus, the left hand must be drafted to the task of line handling while the right handles the rod.

When holding the rod in the right hand and the line in the left, it is difficult to avoid feeding line during the forward stroke. If you permit either hand to approach the other, line feeds out and the cast is partially killed. On the pickup or backcast it is equally difficult to avoid lengthening the distance between your hands. Pulling line in increases the applied force, resulting in unexpected concavity of the flat.

I have known fishermen of many years' experience who have never overcome this simple problem. Oddly enough most of them don't like to be told about it. Such men usually fish well in spite of, rather than because of, what they do, often maintaining that the backcast should be only half as hard as the forward cast. They limit themselves to distance within the range of a half-speed trajectory and encourage others to do likewise.

Anyone who guides fishermen for a number of seasons

will be able to observe numerous fly casters in action, ranging from folks who have never seen a trout to those who have fished from New Zealand to Nova Scotia to Chile to Point Barrow. Among these will be some who welcome help; some who accept it; some who resent it; some who don't need it. In the last group will be the best practical casters and fish handlers in the world; men who have caught tarpon, bonefish, and steelhead on fly tackle. The following instructions are a composite of my observations of such anglers in action.

In coping with a fly line, not only is fast retrieving necessary when fish run toward you, but one must use a safety valve retrieve that will permit the line to slide out again in case the fish is going away when the line comes taut. The method I suggest is the one I consider most suitable for most conditions, assuming that the hooked fish is not more than 100 feet from you. Beyond that distance it usually is better to handle fish with the reel to avoid tangling line.

Let's assume you have made a forward cast and fed some line that will need retrieving before you can pick it up. The first thing to do is reach with your left hand to the first guide on the rod and grasp the line hanging from it, using the left thumb and forefinger. Pull the line along the rod until the thumb and forefinger touch the forward end of the rod grip. Relax and open your RIGHT thumb and forefinger as the line passes, then close them about the line by holding the tips together to form a ring or loop that the line can slide through loosely, like going through another guide, the only difference being that the loop can be closed to hold the line when the finger is pressed against the rod grip.

Continue pulling the line as far as the left hand and arm will reach, letting the line slide through the finger loop. Next tighten the loop to prevent the line from feeding, then reach up with the left hand and pull again. Be sure, this time, to start the left hand *below* the finger loop, *never* above it, except on the original pull. Repeat as many times as necessary to bring the fly within pickup range, then release the line from the finger while still grasping the line with the left hand, grip the rod in the regular way and perform the cast again, holding the line as usual, in the left hand only.

Retrieving Advantages

There are several advantages to this method of retrieve. First, it is faster, for it avoids fumbling for the line. You can always close your eyes and touch your hands together, but it is difficult to find the butt guide on your rod without looking. Second, by holding your rod hand high overhead, or at arm's length to the right, you can bring in five or six feet of line with each stroke of the left arm. This is as much or more than is possible by any other method. Third, your line is grasped by one hand or the other at all times. This prevents the possibility of dropping the line, or otherwise losing control of it. Fourth, it permits you to watch for a fish to strike or for the proper pickup point, instead of watching the line you are handling. Fifth, it permits you to feel, by line tension, exactly what a hooked fish is doing. You won't be quite as surprised by what he does next. Sixth, the gentle grasping of the rod, part of the time with only three fingers, helps prevent "setting" off the fly if you are startled when a fish strikes unexpectedly. And who isn't?

If you are having difficulty with the three-finger grip, the rod handle may be larger than necessary. From the rack of the average dealer, nearly every rod I hold tends to turn over when gripped with three fingers, yet my hand is average size. So, the first thing I do after buying a new rod, or when I build one, is to reduce the size of the cork with sandpaper until the handle doesn't roll when grasped lightly in three fingers. Leaving the cork rough also helps, and I personally prefer a slight oval, like a small hammer handle. My favorite measures $7/8$ in. by $3/4$ in., and this leaves plenty of slack in my finger loop.

Don't blame the manufacturers. Fly rods with large grips usually outsell all others.

Returning to practice, let's assume that you have pulled or "stripped" in line, using your new retrieve. You have picked the line up and now are false casting it, being careful not to let any line slide through your left hand or to LET THE HANDS APPROACH EACH OTHER. The actual distance between them should not vary throughout the series of false casts. Continue false casting until the line held by the left hand seems a normal part of the series.

Now, we must consider varying the length of the false cast. We have been using only 35 feet, the amount established as the best average pickup distance. We may want to reach farther.

When I was a very young guide, I had the opportunity to boat the McKenzie River for a world-famous fisherman, whose prowess had been discussed at length by other guides at the fishing lodge. Baffled that he obviously was not casting the distance of which he was capable, I finally asked how much line a good fly fisherman should use.

"A good fisherman should use enough line to reach from the fisherman to the fish," he replied.

I am sure that I never have heard so much information in so few words. The implication that any weak link in the chain of events can put fish beyond your ability to reach them has been applicable on every trip I have ever taken. The goal of this entire project is to develop your casting beyond any possibility that your cast might become the weakest link in the chain.

When you have become accustomed to false casting with the line held in the left hand, complete a forward cast, letting the line slide through your left hand as it feeds out. Strip it in, roll it, pick it up and repeat the process. This time stop the line from feeding out by closing your left thumb and finger on it. The cast turns over faster than it would if you permitted it to go the full distance. Try this several times until you can stop it consistently when about five feet of line has been fed. Do another backcast, and, instead of letting the line light on the water, continue false casting as before, holding the line at this new distance. The false cast has been lengthened five feet. Since the total distance your fly travels is 10 feet greater, more time will now be required for each cast to turn over. Your timing must be slower to coincide.

Also, you have increased the inertia of the line so the power portion of the stroke must start more gradually. However, it can be lengthened, for the more inertia you have, the more the rod bends, and the more the rod bends, the longer the useable flat spot becomes.

Memorizing the following mottos may be of help:
1. Short line, short stroke—quick timing.
2. Medium line, medium stroke—medium timing.
3. Long line, long stroke—slow timing.

As usual, you should permit the rod to drop after the kill. Start raising it again toward 12 o'clock while the tail is turning over, thus preventing sag in the lag. But there comes a time, as the false casts lengthen, when this technique is not enough. The lag threatens to drop too low in spite of our efforts, simply because the timing has slowed, giving the lag more time to drop. In other words, we now have a trajectory problem.

PUSHING, PULLING THE WHEEL

Reviewing our theory, we find that we have been using the wheel's rotation successfully. Analysis reveals that although we have not been able to use COAM in the rod stroke, we have used it on the turnover at the *other* end of the line by starting the lag in one direction while the tail travels opposite, causing the tail to turn over with greater speed, thus furnishing us with straighter line and more line inertia than we would have had otherwise. But that still leaves us two more useable tools to improve our casting. Let's try the first which consists of moving the axis of our imaginary wheel in the same direction the top of the wheel moves.

While one of the false casts is turning over and you are moving the tip slowly toward 12 o'clock in preparation for the opposite stroke, move your rod hand in the same direction, horizontal with the water and parallel with the false casts. Start your hand slowly, increase the speed gradually as the lag lengthens and end it fast, stopping the force at the kill point, coinciding with the rod stroke. This maneuver, which works equally well in either direction, pushes or pulls the axis of the wheel. The axis travels parallel (horizontal), with the flat spot and is effective only in lengthening the flat beyond its usual boundaries (Fig. 8), permitting more speed at the end. This can be a greater aid than one would guess at first glance. Although the hand moves slowly and although it should be moved only 12 inches or less at first, this method can add many feet to your longest cast. Some casters gain an advantage of four or five feet of flat in this

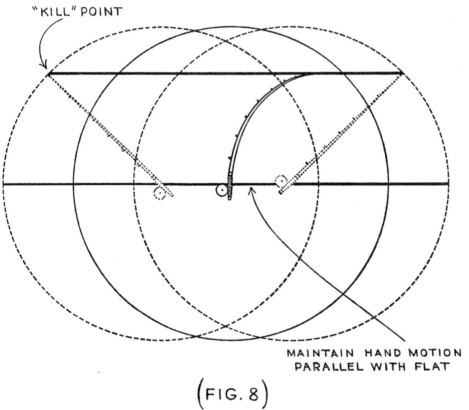

MOVEMENT OF CASTING HAND

"KILL" POINT

MAINTAIN HAND MOTION
PARALLEL WITH FLAT

(FIG. 8)

manner, but it must be done without disturbing the "flat-ness" of the flat—the only limitation. Bear in mind that this should NOT be used at distances that can be reached easily by usual methods. Promiscuous use of this tool encourages any tendency you may have toward tackle fighting. Corrections for errors remain identical with previous casts. Bear in mind that if it doesn't help, you aren't using it properly. Usually the tendency is to OVERDO it.

Increasing Distance

Continuing the practice, we have been false casting about 35 feet and have lengthened that to about 40 feet by letting the line slide through the left hand after the kill point. This does not have to be done in measured five-foot lengths. In fact, it is easier to feed it out in equal amounts on both the forward and backward strokes once you have discovered exactly how to do it. Let's start again with a shorter line and gradually feed out line about a foot at a time until we have difficulty in keeping the backcast off the ground Then, and ONLY then, should the pushing and pulling of the axis be used.

Use it only enough at first to keep the line from drop-ping too low. Very gradually increase the power of both the axis, push-pull, and the rotation, compensating for concavity by lengthening the rod stroke and killing the cast less abruptly. This lengthens the flat still more and helps keep sag out of the lag by creating greater speed which not only gives the lag less time to fall, but furnishes more COAM when the line turns over, helping to pull the lag straight. Since the increased speed of the fly now sends it from one extreme to the other in less time, the timing will have to be speeded up accordingly, compar-

able to a softer and shorter cast. Corrections, except for
concavity will remain the same as usual.

A Distance Ceiling

Using the same length of line, practice building the
power up and cutting it down. Practice time and time
again. Notice that although the forward kill point is
between 10 and 11 o'clock, depending on the weight of
your line, you actually are using some power almost down
to 9 o'clock to avoid concavity at the end of the longer
stroke that would cause the turnover to tangle with the
lag, for, as the flat lengthens, the rod shortens, bringing
the entire flat nearer the axis than previously, and neces-
sitating extra precautionary measures, including a re-
minder that the kill point doesn't necessarily occur when
force stops; only when force LESSENS.

You will be surprised pleasantly to find that with the
added speed, the line can be "shot" much farther when
the left hand releases the slack. With specially con-
structed lines it is possible to shoot nearly as much line
as has been false cast, and the more line you false cast, the
better it will shoot, if you can keep it straight enough.

Next, starting with minimum force, let's gradually
lengthen the line, using more force and more axis motion
only as it is NECESSARY to keep the cast from grounding. Work toward this with caution, for this is the way
to establish the absolute ceiling for a given rod and line.
A ceiling is established by most fishermen when they
reach a point where their own coordination blows up,
rather than the maximum limit of the rod and line.

Cautiously feed more and more line out until it
grounds. If you are casting properly, the backcast should
ground first, because the land behind is higher than the
water in front. Mark the distance by reeling in any slack

between your left hand and the reel, then strip the line in, roll it, pick it up and start all over. This time try pushing and pulling the axis farther. If the line does not ground at the same distance, it indicates that you are using your tackle at near peak efficiency. If it grounds again, your coordination needs polishing. Make certain you are not "bouncing" the axis up and down, for that will cause the whole wheel to bounce, destroying the flatness of the flat, but it might be feasible to try your forward cast over LAND to make certain your forward and backcast are identical.

When your lengthened push and pull begin to pay off, lengthen the line until it grounds again. Repeat with the rod hand above your head, not extended stiffly, but high enough to give you an additional elevation of 12 inches. Used properly, this should enable you to false cast a few feet farther. Continue feeding line out, just inches at a time, until either the line grounds, or the force necessary to prevent it cause the tail and lag to tangle. Try this over and over until one or the other occurs on every cast. Application of any more force beyond the "grounding" accomplishes nothing, and strains the rod unnecessarily. You may feel more comfortable at this point, to prevent possible hazard to your rod, if you make all forward casts over land, and your backcasts over water, for the tackle should rarely, if ever, be used at this distance under actual fishing conditions, for too many tangles result.

Light and Heavy Lines

If you are casting correctly, using only force that is absolutely necessary to prevent the cast from grounding, the threat of tangling of the tail and lag indicates that the tackle is very near its limit with the line you are using.

If you are casting incorrectly, the middle of the lag usually grounds without indicating concavity. Both cases may be helped by switching to a lighter line, or try a stiffer rod to shorten timing and lengthen trajectory. But it is well to bear in mind that a lighter line makes timing more critical.

People who practice in groups of three or more have a distinct advantage, for they have the opportunity to rig three similar rods with three different weights of line and take turns with all three. One rod should be fitted with a line that is heavy for it. In the dry fly class, on an average rod, this would be an HCH double taper or a size C level line, either of which will develop concavity, or ground, before an actual ceiling is reached. The medium would be an HDH double taper, or a size D level, and the light line would be an HEH double taper, an HCF torpedo taper or a size E level line. The level lines are fine for practice if four or five feet of size G level line is spliced on the "leader end" to cushion COAM at the end of the cast. "Mill end" fly levels usually can be bought for a dollar or two. To splice, strip the finish from both sizes for ¾ of an inch, unravel half the distance on each, divide the ends to form a V, overlap the V ends for nearly the full distance of the bare portions, and wrap tightly with thread. Finish with a coat of varnish or household cement. If you want to buy one tapered line, for both practice and fishing, the light torpedo will fit, most nearly, all casting requirements on the average trout rod.

Switching Lines

Beginners in the group should start with the heavier line, which furnishes maximum inertia at a shorter distance, and will do the short rolls with less applied power.

Use the medium until the ceiling is reached by methods covered thus far. If three or four casters agree on the ceiling distance, it will help establish the correct point for changing to a size lighter line. With the medium line, it will usually be a false cast of 45 to 60 feet. To go beyond this ceiling, there are three alternatives leading to greater distances. Either change to a stiffer rod, which will combat concavity when we use more force, or use a lighter line, which will have the same effect as stiffening the rod, or use the "double pull" technique, which will augment the efficiency of either or both.

This technique is the final tool for acceleration of a cast, at least for the present. It first appeared as a "single pull," gaining attention in the early thirties when it was used to break the existing world's distance record, not by mere inches but by nearly 20 feet. Since that time it has been developed by tournament men into the double pull, boosting the record to over 180 feet.

I predict that someday there will be a new champion, possibly one of the basketball greats, a seven-footer who can reach higher for elevation and who can push and pull the axis farther. His hands will have the strength to practice for hours with the stiffest of rods, possibly made from materials with greater initial resistance. Yet, this champion will need vision and coordination that permit hair-trigger timing at long distances; all this so commonplace that tournament tension will not change his emotional stability.

If you think you have a few of these qualities, try tournament work. If you don't have them, join the host of fishermen like me who have just as much fun casting lesser distances with proportionately lighter rods and lines. The only remuneration most of us will ever get

from casting 120 feet is that 75 feet, with a lighter outfit, seems so easy by comparison.

In either case, the double pull will decrease the work
you do. So we should learn it even though we intend to
compete with nothing more than the weather.

Assuming we have reached a ceiling with the rod and
line we have been using, we must now decide either to
switch to a stiffer rod (if our tendency is toward maximum performance) or to a lighter line (if longer hours of
effortless casting are our goal). Since instruction will be
applicable to both (except that tournament applications
are more severe), let's presume that you have chosen the
lighter line.

FOR GREATER DISTANCE

The double pull utilizes the fourth and last tool illustrated in our wheel theory: the shortening of the line itself, while force is being applied (Fig. 9). Just how effective this phase of line acceleration can be depends largely
upon the stiffness of the rod and degree of coordination
possessed by the user. Basically, the longer the cast, the
stiffer the rod must be and the more critical the timing,
for you must use a quick stroke to make the rod bend,
combined with a quick pull of the line, timed precisely
together across the flat, which has the effect of combin-
ing both inertias. The gap between convexity and concavity in tournament quality casting narrows markedly
under these conditions. One cast may turn over, while
the next, that you think is identical, may tangle instead.
This can be overcome by constant practice or by additional line weight. But if the weight (inertia) is in line
diameter instead of in greater length of line, you are defeating your purpose. This drives home the real objective of the fly caster—to get more feet of STRAIGHT

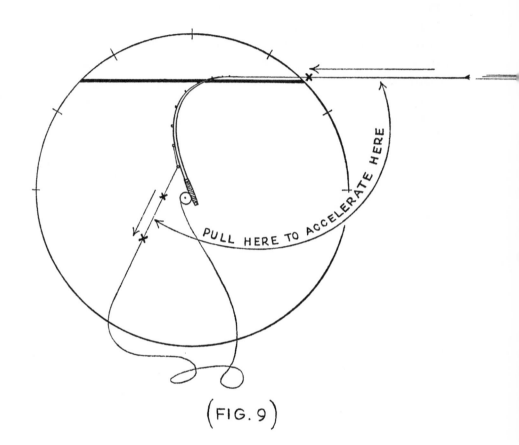

PULL HERE TO ACCELERATE HERE

(FIG. 9)

line following the tip across the flat. This is applicable
to all fly casting and is especially so in long-distance work.
Every foot beyond 100 feet comes just as hard as those
miles per hour over 100 in an automobile. Everything
gets pretty critical, not impossible, but increasingly difficult. Corrections still remain identical. It's the timing
that will get you! Ultimate distance ceilings are governed
by gravity and air resistance alone. The tackle and casting
are variable.

I recall well the first practice group we organized in
my home town of Eugene, Oregon, in 1932. Local mer-
chants had sponsored a tournament with nice prizes for
the top performers. Back in those depression days some
of us really turned on the practice. I had an old one-piece
bamboo rod with a missing portion of tip, broken from
nine feet to eight feet, four inches. It was as stiff as a
board, and since it was useless for anything else, we didn't
mind putting some strain on it. Using two thirds of an
HCH double-tapered line, spliced to some size H shooting line, thoroughly rubbed down with graphite, we did
the practicing on a lawn, without any elevation to stand
on. Within 10 days, with this crude outfit, some of us
were consistently getting 120 feet. The longest cast was
129 feet, which even the champs will say "isn't bad."
When the tournament was held, we were classed as pro-
fessionals and barred from entry, because most of us held
guide licenses. The top prize was awarded for a 70-foot
cast. It was disappointing at the time, but in those ten
days I learned some things about casting that have simplified my problems ever since. I have never felt those
practice sessions wasted. It is seldom that I hold a class
in which some of the novices aren't casting more than 75
feet after 20 hours of instruction.

FOR EASIER CASTING

To consider the double pull in the light of casting ease, under fishing conditions, we must view it in a supporting role rather than as a star performer. As an illustration, let's consider a line which already gives us enough inertia to furnish a flat spot with fairly slow manipulation. Under these conditions an abrupt application of wheel rotation can produce concavity, or an abrupt application of force in pushing or pulling the axis will give the same results. In this instance, pulling the line in, while force is being applied (furnishing still more inertia), makes the matter worse.

Now let's try the same rod with a line light enough so that we must apply force abruptly to both rotation and axis to avoid convexity. Here is a situation with possibilities, for now it will be easier to cast, as the situation occurs in which the double pull will be of advantage. By pulling the line in as maximum force is applied, the other two forces can be relaxed. Thus, the light line casts as easily as the heavier one did previously, and it won't fall as fast, or make as much disturbance when it falls, or is picked up.

Thus, the outfit that was difficult to handle, becomes easy again. In addition, the rod will handle perhaps 60 feet of false cast without concavity, instead of the 40 or 50 feet it handled with the heavier line. The timing is identical, for the fly travels from one extreme to the other in very nearly the same period of time, though the distance is greater. By putting your left hand to work, you have not only lessened the work of the right hand, but you have increased the velocity and lengthened the trajectory of your cast, as well as made the presentation to the fish more delicate. And remember, the longer the false cast, the more slack it will drag out when you release it.

To perform the double pull, start with a standard false cast, fed out to somewhere near the ceiling established for your rod with the heavier line. (If you have a light torpedo line, this would be the time to use it.) Continue false casting, but concentrate for a moment on the portion of the forward stroke before and after the kill point, for you will need to apply force farther than the present kill point, to avoid concavity, because, when you pull line in, the straight line following the tip will "weigh" more.

Just as you gradually start to apply power with your right hand, start moving your left hand gradually toward a point about a foot to the left of your left trouser pocket. Start the motion slowly and end it fairly fast, about the same speed and distance that you have been pushing the axis. After the kill point, bring your left hand back to the original position while the line turns over, feeding the line you have pulled in back out through the guides again.

If the line tangled, you have overdone one of the three forces. If it was aimed too high, or tangled, correct by delaying the kill point. Otherwise, for greater ease, correct by a less forceful but NOT shorter rod stroke, leaving the pull of the line and axis forces the same as before. If the cast was aimed low, your forces were not coincided, which caused convexity, and indicate that you pulled early or late with your left hand. Usually the tendency is to overdo rather than underdo the double pull. I am amazed yet, myself, at the amount of speed that can be gained with such a minimum of effort when the timing is proper. Above all, DON'T TRY HARDER if it doesn't work properly at first. Other corrections remain the same as usual.

Continue false casting, using the single pull on the

forward stroke until you can get the line to turn over with a real "swish" at the end of the cast and the motion of both hands simultaneously seems relaxed and natural. Then, on the backcast give a pull with your left hand identically the same as you have been doing on the forward stroke, bringing the left hand back to its original position while the line turns over. Corrections remain identical with the forward cast. Continue false casting till the procedure becomes familiar.

Graphite for Distance

You are now doing the entire double pull cast, for you are pulling line in and feeding it out again on both the forward and backcasts. If you are using a light torpedo line, you should be able to feed out more than you pull in until you are false casting 15 feet or more beyond your rod's previous false cast ceiling. Your line should drag at least 30 feet of slack with it when you make a final cast, but it might be pertinent to mention that on really long casts, both the tail and lag will be grabbed by gravity, so some power should be applied forward clear to 9 o'clock, so you can slowly pull it back, as the cast turns over, furnishing more COAM when the turnover gets out there a hundred feet or so. Rubbing the shooting portion of the line with graphite is messy, but will get the most distance. Most modern line finishes are smooth enough unless they get gummy from too much line dressing. The shooting portion of a torpedo line should not be dressed heavily or frequently, for it doesn't come in contact with the water often. Some experts treat the tip and "belly" line with dressing and the fine shooting line with graphite only.

An inexpensive line for practicing the double pull can be made as follows: Rig a rod with the size D (for medium) or E (for soft rods) level line on the end of which you already have spliced a piece of finer line to keep it from turning over too fast. False cast it out until it almost grounds. Then, slowly shorten it until you can apply quite a bit of force without getting any concavity. Cut off the line at the tip of the rod and splice about 60 feet of 10- or 12-pound test limp monofilament to the length you have just cut off. To prevent the monofilament from slipping out of the splice, tie a knot in the part that is covered by your wrapping or melt a ball on the end with a match flame.

Hollow *vs.* Solid

You now have a shooting line that will be nearly frictionless, although hard to hang onto. Thread the rod, wind the monofilament on your reel and you are ready for practice, though if left on the reel for long, the monofilament may become curly, and need to be stretched, to perform well. But remember that, although the splice you have made will feed out readily, it will not travel around a sharp corner coming in. Be certain to retrieve with the rod pointing *straight toward the fly as the splice enters the tip guide.* Otherwise, your rod tip may be broken. But, except when landing fish, it is seldom necessary to bring a splice through the tip.

This line will perform well enough to get you 80 or 90 feet with the average trout outfit, and will give you some idea of the size torpedo that best will fit your rod. When buying dry fly lines, remember that the hollow or floater type, weighs less per diameter. A size D "floating line may weigh no more than a size E solid. The more dense a line in relation to its diameter, the better it will cast, but the more difficult it will be to float. This is especially true in the heavier size, partly because it falls faster, frequently breaking the surface tension which keeps any line floating. The recent trend is to designate lines by weight per distance rather than by diameter.

SURFACE TENSION

Surface tension is the property of water which keeps the "greased needle" on the top of water in a glass, and enables insects and spiders to run across the surface of a pond with dry feet. A line held up by surface tension will pick up almost as easily as if it were already airborne. Thus, the "floater" type lines, although actually buoyant, may pick up or roll just as sluggishly as if they were sunken, unless they are dressed (most companies say "cleaned") properly, to take full advantage of surface tension.

In summary, some of the items covered in the preceding several pages, become impossible to perform when the wind blows, unless you know how to use the wind to your advantage. I recommend that these portions be reviewed (starting on page 53) after the chapter on wind casting has been covered.

III.

THE STRATEGY

RECENTLY I HEARD a famous football coach explain the difference between coaching college and professional teams. He described the college job as 90 percent fundamentals and 10 percent strategy, while the pro coaching required 10 percent fundamentals and 90 percent strategy. This is applicable to other sports, especially fishing.

The 90 percent drill on fundamentals came in the preceding pages on theory and practice. Enduring the rigors until now, you should have acquired enough finesse to take you out of the apprentice class. And if there is a dividing line between practice and tactics, it should be drawn when you leave the spot of previous action to seek new locations where varying conditions will prevail.

INTRODUCING WIND CASTING

You will recall that we started the practice session by standing at the edge of a pond, facing west, with the shoreline extending from north to south. A breeze blew from our left, the south shore. Before leaving this spot for new terrain, there are two more experiments to be tried. Both are pertinent to the next phase of casting—"wind" casting.

TURNING FALSE CAST

The first experiment consists of merely performing a series of east and west *right* false casts during which you turn slowly toward north so that instead of a forward and backward series you are doing a left and right series. However, because the palm of your rod hand is toward your face, you continue to think of your right cast to the east as a backcast because you are using a backhand pull to do it. Next, while watching the casts carefully to prevent disturbing the sequence, turn your rod hand *very* slowly until the back of your hand is toward your face. The direction of the false casts should not vary during the turn, and the series should continue afterward.

During the turn, the timing is reversed, so far as your thoughts are concerned. Now the backhand cast goes to the left, toward the west, and by turning your back to the pond your former series of right backcasts to the east have become a series of left forward casts to the east. I doubt that you will be able to discern the exact point at which the changeover occurred. Thus, by using a sort of "Möbius Strip" approach, we have overcome one of the greatest mental hazards ever to plague a fly caster—that of feeling he will not be able to cast on either side of a stream, lake, or boat without making a radical change in casting procedure. And we have proved to ourselves that any actual separation of right and left casts, or forward and backcasts, is purely imaginary.

The maneuver of the turning false cast is one you will use on every trip, especially when fishing from a boat with a heavy breeze blowing. Practice the turn through all distances of false casts, up to the double pull, until your left false casts become thoroughly familiar. Soon we will move to a location where only left casts will work well.

There is one infallible rule of the turning false cast. It must always be performed in such a manner that the line passes the rod on the downwind side. To illustrate this I have devised the second experiment, which should not be tried without adequate eye protection.

It begins with an ordinary series of comfortably short false casts while facing west. When you have the series timed so you can continue without watching, look directly up the rod to the tip. If there is much of a breeze blowing, the tail of the line will be passing the rod some distance north of the path the rod tip follows. Tilt the rod farther away from the wind, and notice that the distance between the rod and line increases. Return it to its original path and notice that it narrows again.

Continuing the series, try pointing the rod so that the imaginary wheel is precisely vertical, and the rod tip passes directly overhead. If the breeze still blows, the line still passes the rod on the downwind or north side. If the breeze stops, the tail will pass directly over the route taken by the rod. However, it still clears the tip without tangling if you are casting without concavity.

But now continue the series, and at the same time gradually tilt the top of the wheel toward the south, into the wind. You will notice that the tail continues to approach the rod, closer and closer, but it also swoops lower and lower as the rod tip loses altitude, but the line loses it faster, until the paths of the rod and line coincide, resulting in a tangle. They tangle, that is, unless the tail already has wrapped itself around your neck. Why should the tail tangle with the rod when tilted into the wind, if it didn't tangle on the overhead cast during which the rod apparently was elevated higher, and thus should have been more directly in the path of the line?

It's a good question, with a good answer, simply that the approaching wind can push harder sideways on a cast than gravity can pull downward on an overhead cast. In other words, the wind may cause it to drift faster than it normally would fall during an overhead cast.

For example, let's say you are sidecasting 50 feet with a 10-foot rod, with the rod pointed against the wind. If your fly is traveling 50 miles per hour, then a 10 mile per hour cross wind will cause the tail to drift in ten feet across the axis and hook you. Of course, we can increase the velocity of the fly by using more force, but there isn't any guarantee by the weather bureau that the wind velocity won't suddenly increase, too. If so, the fly will pop you harder.

In case an overhead cast doesn't turn over, or you can't build much inertia because the line is not straight enough, convexity is indicated, corrected by use of more force and a shorter stroke. This same treatment will correct your troubles now, until the wind dies suddenly. Then, as you build more inertia than you expect, the flat becomes concave and the tail again cuts across the axis. This time the fly *really* will pop you. And because the slackening of the wind affects the cast several seconds before you are aware of it, you have no warning of the approach of the "uninvited guest."

The chain of events described above probably has been occurring ever since the first fly caster tried to cast with his rod tilted toward the wind. It is likely to reoccur any time you attempt it. It is never more reliable than the wind itself.

Descending without a hint of warning, the fly suddenly explodes in the caster's face, frequently catching him with his eyes wide open. I think that 99 percent of all serious accidents in fly casting result directly from failure to recognize and abide by this one rule imposed on us by nature in the form of a perfectly normal breeze.

To avoid this hazard, establish which direction the

breeze is coming from, turn your back toward it, and then cast across wind (Figs. 7 and 10). This will be explained further in subsequent pages.

POINTING AWAY FROM THE WIND

For contrast, lets' turn to face away from the wind and study what it does to our casting.

Holding the rod at north, we find the wind has no effect, but if we move it either east or west, we meet wind resistance, causing some rod curvature. In this situation both the forward and backward casts are against the wind, indicating that force should be applied later and the kill point delayed in both directions, because 9 o'clock and 3 o'clock are not where they were previously.

When force is applied so late in the stroke, sudden failure of the wind results in convexity, widening the turnover and causing the tail of the line to pass farther from us than ever. This actually increases the margin of safety.

Viewing an imaginary circle from the exact center where we stand, we find that a strong gust of wind instantly causes half of the circle to become difficult to cast in, leaving only the downwind half in which it is safe and easy to cast.

GOOD, BAD HALVES

For the sake of simplicity, I will refer to these half circles as the easy or "good" half and the difficult or "bad" half (Fig. 10). This does not mean that casts cannot be made into the bad half, but they will be more difficult because the wind blows slack into the line, defeating inertia, while in the good half, wind blows the line straighter, helping to build inertia. Thus, it isn't the cast going into the bad half, but the pickup coming out that is dif-

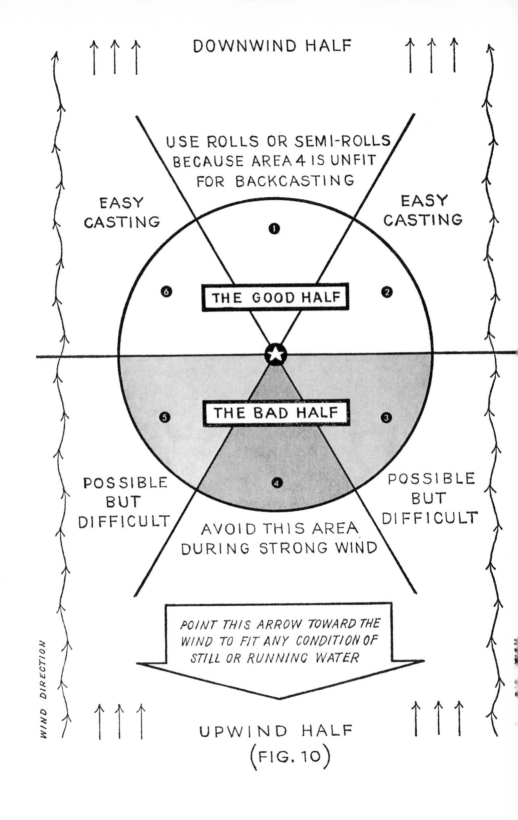

(FIG. 10)

ficult if not actually dangerous. For this reason, I always perform a roll before the pickup. If you roll or cross cast your line into the good half before false casting, you probably will never hook yourself.

Tilting the Turnover

If you have followed my suggestions regarding approach of the pond in relation to wind, you have been performing nearly all of your casting in the good half, although the rod has been tilted only slightly away from the wind.

Next, let's experiment with a side cast instead of one overhead. This will work well when the wind is strong for the wind helps straighten the line and holds it up, compensating for any lack of elevation. Start with a series of normal false casts and, without pausing, gradually tilt the top of the wheel toward north. Somewhere between the vertical and a point shoulder high at north, you will find a plane where the false casts work easier, though a longer than usual stroke is necessary. Not only are you better able to feel the weight of the line, but the fly doesn't seem to drift as badly after it turns over. Searching for an explanation, we find that the turnover now is tilted in the same plane as the wheel. The cast *turns over* at the end, and the fly, affected by COAM once more travels against and into the wind, straightening the line and resulting in more inertia. All adds up to easier casting.

Avoid Breaking Hooks

Following the theory of tilting the turnover, let's see if we can apply it usefully in eliminating the bane of waders, the breaking of hook points on the rocks behind. This is a genuine hazard, not mental. Rare, indeed, is the fisherman who cannot recall a tremendous fish that rose to a fly with no point, or a time when the only fly a fish would strike, was ruined by having the point knocked off. The entire blame for such a miscarriage of justice can be charged to COAM. Its effect, as the turnover reaches the end of the line, is so great that it can easily break fly hooks which otherwise could be dropped a hundred miles without damage.

With an overhead cast we are taking this risk any time we use enough line to threaten grounding on the backcast, for the COAM of the turnover projects the fly downward at the end of the cast with fantastic speed. If we could, we should devise a cast that would cause the lag to form ABOVE the tail, like the roll, for then, the turnover and COAM should project the fly *upward* instead of *downward*.

To accomplish this, we know that after maximum power has been applied the rod must be raised above the path the tail will follow. The most plausible method would be to pick up and backcast to the side, then raise the rod after the kill point, and do the forward cast overhead. Referring back to theory, we hold the wheel flat on the backcast and then tilt the wheel vertical for the forward cast. Practicing a series of false casts in this manner, we find that the backcasts *do* turn *up* at the end instead of down. Sufficient practice of this maneuver will cause the capsule-shaped path of the rod tip to seem entirely normal, ending forever the nuisance of hooks broken on gravel bars behind you. All you can hit this way is birds and bats.

WITH THE WIND FROM THE RIGHT SIDE

Moving to a spot directly across the pond, we face east, and the backcast will be toward the west. Before starting to cast, we must ALWAYS notice the direction of the wind and establish the good and bad halves.

If the wind continues from the south, the bad half is on our right, eliminating false casting on that side. All false casts must be either left casts or right backhand casts. To become more accustomed to this, start a series of left false casts. Without pausing, slowly turn your back to the pond until the left false casts have become right false casts.

Continue without pausing as you slowly turn back to face the pond again. Still without pausing, lengthen the line a few feet and repeat the entire procedure. Continue through all distances to (and including) a mild application of the double pull. If casting with your back to the pond seems more natural, it will help some to hold the rod higher overhead while facing the pond, for it isn't essential that the rod be held on your left side, merely that the line PASSES on your left side. However, if there are obstructions behind, such as trees with small gaps between them, it is actually better to aim your forward cast toward the point of *greatest hazard* because it is easier to watch. So, turning your back to the water, you direct your forward cast west into a space between trees, letting your backhand cast to the east light in the pond instead. Neither your rod nor the fish will notice any difference, and you have eliminated the possibility of fouling your fly in the trees.

Remember your line usually goes where you look. Be sure to gaze at the *space between* the trees and not at the trees themselves.

FACING THE WIND

Our next position is on the north side of the pond, facing the wind from the south (Fig. 7). Now all available fishing area is in the bad half of the circle. All casts over the water must be harder and lower than usual, and all casts over land must be higher and softer. The variation will be least noticeable the more nearly east and west we cast. But it will be at a maximum north and south, in Areas 1 and 4.

When we cast directly south into the wind, the back false cast or pickup will be dangerous. To prevent the tail from coming straight at us, we should use the side backcast and the overhead forward cast, using 6 and 3 or 5 and 2 rather than 1 and 4. In a final cast, if it does not turn over, it should be rolled east or west without being picked up. Use of the single pull on the forward cast will help turn it over in extreme wind. The backcast won't need it, because the wind will help straighten and support it.

All casts to the left of the wind should be left casts (Areas 6 and 3), with the rod tilted to the left (north), so that the wind blows the tail from you as it passes. All casts to the right should be right casts (Areas 5 and 2), tilted to the right (north) for the same reason.

In addition to being difficult, this location is not usually very productive because the wind tends to carry insects away from the water rather than toward it.

Don't expect too much distance against the wind. A cast of 50 or 60 feet is plenty for an average outfit. The chief nuisance occurs when the wind blows the fly back through the leader loop (turnover) instead of turning over, usually tying a little single knot, referred to by various unprintable monickers, that will break easily, causing you to lose your best fish. For this reason, you should avoid casting directly into the wind, if possible. If not, be sure to shorten your line until it turns over with force to spare on each cast. COAM can be accented by pulling back more sharply just as the cast turns over. For safety, his should be used only on final casts. Aim all casts low so the wind will not have time to drift them after they turn over. Any extra commotion won't be noticed by the fish due to surface turbulence caused by the wind, because you are on the downwind side of whatever body of water you are fishing, which is always the roughest side.

With the Wind from Behind

The last position will be at the south side of the pond. Here we face the water to the north with the wind coming directly from behind. All of the water in front of us is in the good half. It seems that we could do no wrong by avoiding backcasts. Testing this, let's try some rolls, making the turnovers high, to let the wind help us. As usual, we use right rolls to move our casts to the left, until we reach northwest. There the right backcast to the southeast (Areas 3 and 6) will be at enough angle across the wind to be safe to handle. The same would be true of left casts from northeast to southwest and return (Areas 2 and 5). In either case the wind will drift the line away from us. But we still must shun a backcast straight into the wind (Area 4), where a possible neutralizing of COAM by the wind might let the lag fall, taking the tail with it. This threatens our anatomy on the next forward cast, since there is no method of determining where the fly may be when the forward cast is started. But there is a "remedy"—the "semi-roll" cast.

The Semi-Roll Cast

This is one more valuable maneuver to be learned before leaving the pond. Our false casts to northwest or northeast give us a chance to reach maximum distances, but casts due north have been limited to roll distance, because we cannot safely use a south backcast.

North distance (Area 1) can be increased by a maneuver I refer to as a semi-roll. It starts just like a regular side pickup. As soon as the fly leaves the water, the cast should be killed so that the fly and part of the tail land in the water again, about halfway in from the original distance. After the kill, the rod should continue without pausing into an overhead forward cast, just as soon as the tail has touched in front long enough to be *anchored*. The forward cast must be executed before the loop of line behind has time to fall. If the fly picks up and comes toward you, the applied force was a trifle early, before anchoring was adequate. Killing the pickup sooner or using more line will compensate for this. If it did not turn over, you were anchored too deeply. More force is needed, but keep the stroke fairly short, aiming the cast high for the wind to catch. In still weather, it will go farther if aimed lower, and if used against the wind it can be done with a side stroke, if necessary. Considerably more distance can be cast with the semi-roll than with a regular roll, because you can build more straight-line inertia. It is valuable to know the semi-roll when trees are close enough to prevent a full backcast. When you have it working properly, try about three in succession, feeding some line after the kill on each. Because they won't have time to anchor much, you will be able to pick up at a greater distance than with the regular roll. Give the last one a good application of the single pull, aiming it high so the wind catches it, and feed it plenty of slack after the kill. You will be surprised at the distance you get, especially with a torpedo line. The semi-roll is also of distinct advantage in getting a long cast off the water to relocate over rapidly cruising fish. If the first roll doesn't lift cleanly, use a semi-roll, then a regular pickup.

FROM STILL TO RUNNING WATER

Now let's move to a stream, where currents will have an effect on our casting.

We approach the stream from the east side, facing west, with the breeze still coming from the south. For purposes of illustration, the stream should have some current near the shore, gradually increasing to the center, which we will assume is the distance of your longest casts. With the current flowing from north to south, it approaches from your right and flows away to the left. The good half for casting is to the right and the bad half is to the left. (Coincide Figure 10 with Figures 11, 12, 13 and 14, with the * representing the caster in each instance.)

WITH THE WIND FROM THE LEFT—(FACING WEST)

The first difference we notice between pond and stream is that the line we cast out is swept into the bad half by the current. Regardless of the direction of a cast, the retrieve and pickup will always *drift into, and need to be retrieved* from, the *bad half,* requiring special precautions. This in turn indicates that we should limit our normal pickups at southwest. From there to south, it will be safer and easier to use a left cross cast (starting with the rod pointed southeast) to the northwest, followed by a right pickup and right false casts east and west, which will be across the wind. With practice you will be able to perform this maneuver without letting the fly touch the water at northwest, going directly from the left cross cast into the right false casts without a pickup. But don't try this at first, for the timing is rather critical.

In case there are trees or a high bank behind you, the

left cross cast to northwest can be followed by either a right roll or a right semi-roll to west, instead of the regular pickup, being certain not to cross line in the water with your roll.

Any of these maneuvers will get your fly into the proper direction, which, for dry fishing, usually is somewhere upstream from a line drawn at right angles to the current flow (Fig. 11). This helps eliminate the triple curse of the "dragging" fly, the disturbance caused by it, and the fact that fish usually will miss a fly that accelerates.

A Careless Approach

It is always good tactics to fish "close" at first, for there is a "mental hazard" that makes most of us feel there should be better fishing on the far side of the stream, resulting from the fact that on previous trips, the fish on the near side were "spooked" before they were covered properly. Some 90 percent of wading fishermen enter water where they should be fishing, using more line than they should handle, attempting to reach a spot on the far side of the current exactly like the one they are standing in.

Never ignore the close water or underestimate the importance of the approach. This was the chief reason for starting you casting with your hand alone. A moving rod and line don't create much of a shadow, but moving hands and arms do. If you don't believe it, try fishing for bullfrogs.

In most situations, if you cast a long line at the start, you will *have* to cast a long line to reach the fish. This reminds me of an incident many years ago, when Guy Kibbee informed a group of guides at lunchtime that if we never drank anything stronger than milk, we never would have to drink milk.

INTRODUCTION TO DRAG

Starting close in and gradually working toward the center, we find that a cast in the same direction each time is actually covering as much area as casts in several directions would accomplish on a pond, but the current carries our line around to south each time, creating a drag that either causes the fly to sink or to pull rapidly on the surface, with the line preceding the fly and making a very unnatural disturbance, and finally whipping around, straight, at south. Assuming that a fish would have to be pretty gullible to be attracted by an insect performing in this manner, we must improvise corrective methods.

CURRENT LEAD

The necessary correction can be illustrated best by picturing three men holding a piece of rope. One stands on the near curb of a street; one in the center; one on the opposite curb. If all three walk in the same direction at the same speed, the rope remains straight. If the man on the near curb stops, the man on the far end will not only be pulled off the curb, but in order to keep the rope in a straight line, will have to walk twice as fast as the man in the center. If we substitute our rod, line, and fly for the three men, we can establish that dragging of the fly can be prevented by having the "near curb man" (B, Fig. 12, which in this instance is the rod tip) travel with the current at the same speed the current and fly (1, Fig. 12) (other men) travel. So, we must always move the rod upstream as soon as the cast is killed, but before any part of the line touches the water, and then move the rod downstream so that the segment of line between the rod tip and the water hangs STRAIGHT DOWN, after the line alights on the water, following the current with the rod as the line and fly float along (to Points C and 2) , fig-

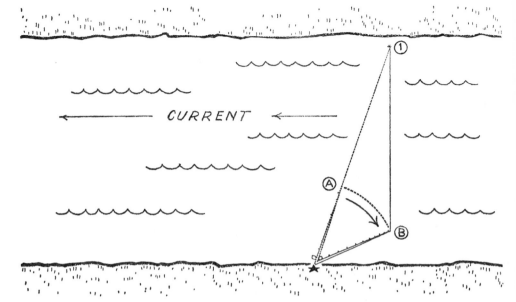

AFTER FINAL CAST KILL POINT, ROD IS MOVED FROM Ⓐ TO Ⓑ AND LOWERED AS FLY ALIGHTS AT ①

(FIG. 11) "CURRENT LEAD"

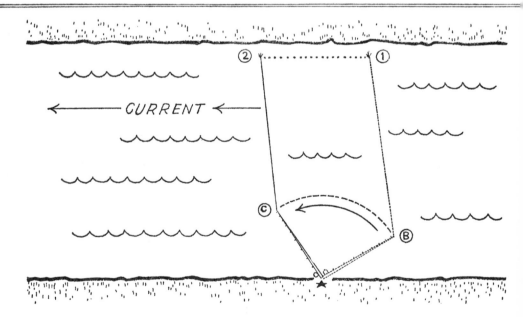

AS FLY FLOATS FROM ① TO ②, ROD TIP IS MOVED FROM Ⓑ TO Ⓒ, PREVENTING FLY FROM EXCEEDING CURRENT SPEED

(FIG. 12) "CURRENT LEAD"

ure 12. This maneuver will be referred to as "current lead" because you are leading on the speed of the current in the same manner that a hunter leads on the flight speed of a duck or pheasant. It will get you nearly two rod lengths of "dead float" under almost any conditions, if your line and fly alight on the water at the same time.

Of course, the "middle man" will pull the "far man" off the curb if your line alights *before* the fly and floats downstream *ahead* of it. After the final cast the rod tip should be held within a foot or two of the water throughout the float, and a rising fish should be set by jerking *upstream against the current, without elevating the rod,* to prevent a floating line from lifting off the water, thus spoiling the shock of the "set."

THE REFLOAT

Current lead can be used to advantage on any cast from the most simple roll to the longest pull cast. However, it will be effective only for a maximum dead float of two rod lengths when casting straight across the current. More float can be obtained by casting more diagonally upstream, for the distance between the "curb men" lessens then, slackening the rope so that there is no pull on either end. However, the fly eventually will drag in either instance. Since it seems a waste of energy to cast three times the distance your fly will float eventually, we need a system to keep it looking natural until it swings around to south.

I believe that this maneuver, which I call the "refloat," was first developed on the McKenzie River, although it is allied to the European "mend." It is used when fishing two dry flies or a dry "drop" or a wet "end" fly, though it also embodies some of the merits of both the wet-fly "action retrieve" and the actual pickup and recast. Used properly it is more deadly than any of the three, for it permits more action of the fly and longer floats than the mend, and it permits dead float, or action retrieve, or the use of current lead repeatedly, without the necessity of recasting.

It was an outgrowth of necessity, for on the McKenzie, during some hatches, we cast all day from fast water, where the boat is being held, into slow water along the banks. Under these conditions, the current instantly grabs the line, requiring repeated applications of current lead and refloat to keep the fly within reach of the fish, and prevent pulling it too far from the shoreline too abruptly. These conditions are responsible for the widespread use of two flies on the leader. In addition to its attraction, the top one becomes an indicator to aid in proper refloating.

In order to understand the refloat thoroughly, first we should analyze the conditions that make it necessary. Let's have two curb men stand side by side on the same curb, each holding one end of the rope, while the center man stays in the street, pulling the middle of the rope toward the opposite curb. When the rope comes taut, one of the curb men drops the rope, while the other retains his hold. If the center man permits the rope to slide through his hand as he continues to the far curb, he will find that the loose end of rope catches up with him at that point, indicating that the loose end has been traveling *twice* as fast as the man was walking, and that a fly in similar circumstances would travel twice as fast downstream as the current and line, especially when casting at an angle upstream.

Thus the very principle that keeps the "tail" from falling when we cast, hinders our fishing when the line is on the water. Unfortunately, the fish, always facing upstream in a current, will see the line approaching before the flies come in sight. To avoid this, use the refloat, for it will offer the flies to the fish before they have an opportunity to find fault with the line or leader.

THE REFLOAT CONTINUED

To go through the entire procedure, let's begin with the line at cross cast distance downstream at south, with two flies on our tapered leader, about four and a half feet apart. The top, or "dropper" fly should be fastened to the main leader by a piece of the same material as the fine end of the leader. The fly should be an easily visible color, and dressed well so it floats "fluffy" dry. The end fly may be anything that matches available food in the area. Books could be written, and many have been, on choices of flies, and why, but that will be covered briefly in subsequent pages.

Assuming that we are in our original position on the stream, facing west, let's do a cross cast to the northwest, a right pickup and backcast to east, and a final cast about a rod's length north of west, moving the rod tip toward northwest for current lead while the line turns over. (Fig. 11). Drop the rod tip as the line and fly drop, and follow the line downstream with the rod tip to avoid drag (Fig. 12). Watch the drop fly, and when it begins to drag (or just before) raise the rod just as though you were going to pick up, increasing the lift gradually, and moving the tip upstream for current lead (Fig. 13). Continue the motion until the drop fly lifts off the water and moves upstream from the end fly, then drop the tip abruptly, straight downward, so that the end fly remains as nearly anchored in its original location as possible (Fig. 14). This will completely straighten the line between the rod tip and the flies, as well as *renew the*

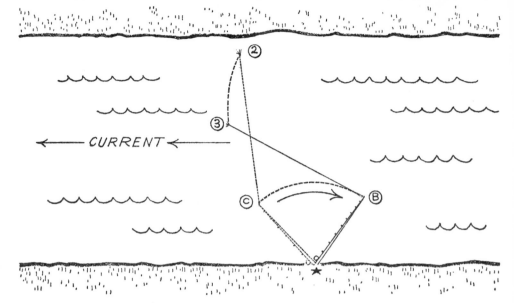

ROD IS RAISED FROM Ⓒ AND DROPPED AT Ⓑ,
FLY MOVES FROM ② TO ③

(FIG.13) "REFLOAT"

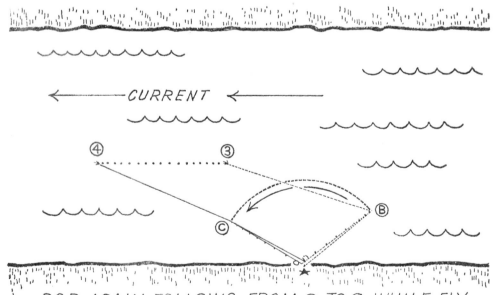

ROD AGAIN FOLLOWS FROM Ⓑ TO Ⓒ WHILE-FLY
FLOATS FROM ③ TO ④...REPEAT AS OFTEN
AS NECESSARY TO COVER ENTIRE AREA

(FIG.14) "REFLOAT"

current lead, fig. 14 (B to C and 3 to 4), if done properly. With very light lines, the end fly will merely do an "about face" in place, and no more deadly action than this can be applied to any fly. With medium lines, the end fly will drag in toward you a few feet, but still appears quite attractive from a "fish-eye view." The heavier lines cannot be anchored adequately by a mere fly in the water, thus the extra distance you are able to cast with a stiff rod and heavy line is partly neutralized when fishing a current, by the fact that you cannot manipulate the fly properly after you get it out there. This is especially true of heavy double-tapered lines, and is probably responsible for my preference for the light torpedo taper, which permits line to be "fed out" after the current lead has been "used up," permitting the fly to float indefinitely without drag. I have seen fish hooked nearly fifty yards below the boat when using this method. At least one American company now makes torpedoes, in sizes down to HEG.

WARNING OF UNEXPECTED STRIKES

It might be timely here to warn you to expect a sudden strike just as you are finishing a refloat with very light equipment (Fig. 14, B and 3). The fish usually thinks one fly has just flown away, and the second one is about to; consequently he will blast it just as you are lowering the rod, and it requires a bit of alertness to stop the downward motion of the rod and jerk upstream instead. Some days, the fish seem intentionally to wait for this, and there doesn't seem to be any restrictive law to deprive them of the privilege. They apparently reserve the right to think you are "fishing" any time your fly is on the water, despite either individual or mass disapproval. Thus, there is no substitute for alertness, or any real excuse for a lack of it.

Necessity of "Setting" the Hook

While we are on the subject of "setting" the hook, I should probably mention that I have seen fish take a floating fly many thousands of times during my years as a professional guide. Many hundreds of times this has occurred while the fisherman was not watching. Yet I have NEVER seen a fish hooked on a floating fly, without intentional manipulation of the rod to "set" the hook. NOT ONE SOLITARY EXCEPTION.

However, I repeatedly hear and read of nationally known authorities who maintain that "setting" the hook is entirely unnecessary, and that the fish hook themselves when they close their mouths. Yet, you can take the same fly, on the same slack leader, and open and close your hand on it all day, if you like, without any risk of hooking yourself. I don't know if these authorities have their hooks trained better than ours, or whether our underprivileged Western rainbow trout are resentful for never having been exposed to such cooperative philosophy. In any event I am convinced that the trout of the McKenzie are entitled to the unofficial spitting championship of the world. And they certainly don't close their jaws hard enough on an insect to drive a hook point in to the hilt. That much force requires quite a jolt.

Even when retrieving wet flies, the only fish that can be hooked without a "set" are those that strike "going away." Your percentage may be good on the number of strikes you get, but it also indicates that you may have created an area of disturbance that the fish are inclined to shun, and you are only getting a percentage of the strikes you should. Thus you are not covering the water at peak efficiency. The old "Grandads" usually won't fall for that kind of an approach, and they are the ones most likely to coast on toward you after striking. Consequently, when a fish strikes, I jerk. I think you should jerk. It should be a jerk abrupt enough to cause the line to run around curves in the current as if it were traveling around pulleys, but only far enough to cause the fly to move suddenly for three of four inches. Then tighten the line as if you were going to do a side pickup until the desired tension is gained. On long casts, or fish that run *toward you,* stripping will be necessary. You should practice the set, and observe results, on nearly every cast during practice to become accustomed to the proper force at varying distances. Fish under twelve inches may be set as soon as they are seen on a dry fly, but larger fish, which are easier to see under the water, should not be set until their noses *point downhill.* Before that point their mouths may be open, causing them to hook thin or be missed entirely.

Different outfits will vary on the amount of time lag between your own force on the grip and actual movement of the fly, involving a rod characteristic which I will refer to as "initial" or "early" resistance. Initial resistance is the quality of a rod material that causes it to resist bending as soon as force FIRST STARTS to be applied, and must not be confused with actual stiffness. Two apparently identical rods may bend the same amount with a certain amount of line pull, yet at half the amount of bend, one may still pull almost as hard, while the other may nearly let the line fall slack. The first rod would be far superior to the second in this instance, for the tip responds more immediately and accurately to whatever your hand dictates. This is at least partially a characteristic of the actual material in a rod, though variations in rod taper and line weight can accent or nullify its effectiveness. We will consider this later during rod comparisons.

LEFT REFLOAT AND CURRENT LEAD

Returning to the river, we have completed a refloat with current lead. As soon as drag threatens, repeat the whole procedure, again and again, until the line is far enough south to permit another cross cast into the good half. When this becomes familiar, we are ready to go across the river and take up a similar location on the west side.

Here we find that the good half is all on our left side, so our false casts must be left casts; the refloat and current lead accomplished by moving the rod upstream to the left. Fish must also be set to the left, with the tip low. Since we are facing the stream, toward the east, the sun will be at our backs in the afternoon, which makes visibility easier, but may cause our lengthening shadow to spook our fish unless we approach each position with caution. This is partly responsible for the conclusion, eventually arrived at by most fishermen, that fly fishing is better after sunset; a conclusion not always supported by fact.

HANDLING A DOWNSTREAM WIND

Before going into tackle analysis, we should probably consider the possibility of wind blowing downstream so the good half is also downstream from us. This is not a productive situation on our western streams, usually indicating dropping temperature, and increasing pressure, as well as making it difficult to hold a boat properly, but since we are sometimes victims of this circumstance, we should be able at least to cope with its mechanical aspects.

Basically, all preliminary casts into the bad half should be either rolls or crosses, and false casts, across the wind as usual. The refloat and current lead become more important than ever, but should be used less often with longer floats between because any insect rising from the water will be blown downstream; a phenomenon that cannot be artificially duplicated without your line covering the fish before your flies do.

Wind blowing across the river, from either side, may be handled the same as it was on the pond under similar conditions.

Choosing Tackle

At this point, let's consider variations in tackle, and some of the good and bad features. I don't recall ever seeing any tackle advertised as other than the best, seldom qualified as best to "cast with," best "for the price," or best thrown overboard. Advertising can therefore be quite confusing, so I will attempt once again to indicate the things that must be accomplished in taking fish so that you may choose gear that fits your specific needs.

In considering tackle comparisons, it should be thoroughly understood that there is no such thing as an ideal outfit. I have always wanted an automobile that would haul a heavy trailer up steep grades without shifting, that would go one hundred miles per hour, get sixty to seventy miles per gallon of fuel, and cost around two hundred bucks, brand new. Car owners in general will, of course, realize the absurdity of this, and most of them can explain, in considerable detail, just why my wish will never come true. Yet many of these same folks expect the fly outfit they buy to cast long distances effortlessly, pick up or drop the line on the water without disturbance, possess great "power" with easy timing, and give years of trouble-free performance, all for about ten dollars total cost. To those who know tackle, the last example is just as absurd as the first.

For some perverse reason, the guys with hands like a gorilla will often choose a rod like a fairy wand, then try to lift a two-pound fish into the boat with it, while the light slender men seem to prefer seven ounce ten-foot rods, that most of them can't move fast enough to set their fish properly. There are, of course, exceptions, occurring often enough that I almost refuse to build a rod for a fisherman until I have watched him cast, for some small men are very strong, and some big fellows could catch tossed beads with a hatpin. Consequently, for many years, I have owned rods in every category, furnishing rods for new fishermen to cast with so I can observe their tendencies and recommend gear that will suit their individual abilities more precisely. This has cost me a few dimes, but it has been interesting research, and I feel that in many instances I have simplified their problems, while I have, to a degree, been recompensed from a guide's viewpoint, by shorter working hours because my fishermen were performing more efficiently.

ONE ROD OR MORE?

For fishermen who must limit themselves to one outfit, I suppose the nearest thing to a happy medium for the average caster would be an eight and a half or nine foot rod, not very stiff, fitted with an HDH double taper or HCF torpedo. But for fishermen here in Oregon, two rods are almost a necessity. For boat fishing the rivers, for trout, where your rods and flies are in almost constant motion, my personal favorite is a seven and a half footer, weighing three or four ounces at nine a.m., and by dusk, it will often seem like ten pounds, unless you rest more or are much tougher than I.

But there are also times when we fish less intensively, and for heavier fish. Here, the little wisp becomes pitifully inadequate. Fly fishing for striped bass or salmon in salt water, for winter or summer steelhead using weighted flies, for bass bug casting, or working the larger lakes for large Browns and Rainbow, a heavier rod is essential. The larger and more exposed a body of water is, the more severe the wind is likely to be, therefore a rod that can shoot out a hundred feet between gusts, and let you relax for five minutes while retrieving it, will be no more tiring than a lighter one, though this is the only advantage a heavy rod has over a light one in the wind if other ratios are equal. For this kind of fishing a nine and a half, or even a ten foot rod is fine. If it is to be used occasionally in salt water, corrosion-proof guides are an absolute must.

These two rods would fill my requirements quite well. However I do not necessarily recommend them for others. Both of them have good and bad features.

LIGHTER RODS

Let's consider the merits of light tackle first. Light rods, using lighter lines and leaders, permit greater stealth in your approach, and their flexibility lessens the danger of setting flies off with light leaders, or tearing small hooks out of a fish's mouth. Light lines refloat beautifully, and since they taper less abruptly they fall at more uniform speed throughout their length when cast, which helps their floating qualities. The light rod is a joy to handle fish on, for a pound fish will give you a real battle. Frequently a light line can be floated or refloated over rising fish repeatedly without putting them down. Thus you are permitted to change flies until you find exactly the right one. Old, wise fish are more apt to be fooled by light gear, and often a limit can be taken from a single riffle or pool during a good hatch. In still weather, or during a hatch that occurs on glassy water, the light gear will take fish when all else fails, and you can use it day after day without danger of a lame wrist or "tennis elbow." Because it keeps a more even tension on hooked fish, by arching more with a given grip pressure, fewer fish will be lost after being hooked properly. Timing of the cast is never very critical, for the tail is so light it follows the turnover from almost any angle, and fewer barbs will be knocked off on rocks behind you because COAM is less severe. Light rods, usually shorter, are easier to carry and store.

On the demerit side, light rods are definitely more fragile, and easier for careless hands to ruin, especially if too heavy a line is used. Light lines must be stripped in closer to roll and pick up, and light leaders are more prone to tangle on a windy day. Neither do they turn over as well when casting against the wind, for they fall more slowly, after turning over, and consequently drift more. Light leaders will fool more big fish, but the "big one gets away" more often too, if your gear isn't adequate to cope with his range and speed. When using tackle too light to "fit the fish," a hooked fish will frequently sulk for long periods instead of putting on a spectacular show. Light rods lack the distance to battle heavy winds and water conditions where the long cast and retrieve pay the dividends by covering a greater area in less time when fishing at random or in strange waters. The light outfit will not turn over properly while using heavy or bulky flies, except when cross cast, or will it set hooks well when the line is deeply sunken or too long. So much for light gear.

HEAVY RODS

The best point of the heavy rod is, of course, its ability to get distance and to take a beating. From the latter standpoint, the fiberglass rods are probably more practical, though top grade bamboo is my choice in the lighter weights if the prices don't scare you.

The greater distance gained with heavy gear enables you to use larger flies, which permits you to match "hatches" other than actual insects. Frogs, mice, tadpoles, small birds, crawfish, leeches, shrimp, squids and small crabs, as well as all kinds of small fish, can be matched and cast with the heavy fly rod, sometimes with greater efficiency than the natural baits would have, for you can cover more area in less time if you are tough enough. Heavy gear will roll cast much better, and a ten-foot rod can give you enough extra elevation, when you are wading waist deep, to almost double your distance. Also, the heavier lines will sink faster, enabling you to retrieve faster, or more often, and still maintain a given depth when fishing deep and wet. When your boat is anchored, the big rod will give you more chances as a feeding fish cruises past, for he will be within casting range longer, and if some old socker leaps ten or twelve feet straight toward you, after being hooked, you have a better chance of keeping the line taut with the longer rod.

Conversely, the big rod is a tiring tool, and it gets monotonous casting your top distance unless it is paying its way. Thus you should have the fish located, the hatch time established, and the hatch itself matched, before the big rod will work at top efficiency without being a drudge. and these conditions are the exception rather than the rule for the casual fisherman. Also, this is, in itself, a paradox, for if you have these conditions under control, the light rod will be more fun and more effective, under average conditions, than the heavy one.

Heavier lines are notorious "water killers," and in boat guiding I have often seen "synthetic experts," with heavy rods, effectively and methodically kill the water, before their partners, using lighter outfits, had any chance of reaching it. Frequently, in such instances, light outfits, used carefully, could have been quite productive.

Also, when you are tired, there is more lag, or lost time, between the reactions of the eye and the hand; thus there will be times when you see a fish rise, but your hand doesn't respond instantly because of fatigue. An attempt to hurry results in the use of more force (which in turn results in more "follow through") , which inevitably sets flies off in fish. This can be countered when dry fly fishing by permitting the rod to lie lightly across the palm of your left hand when expecting a strike; then tilting the rod upward by raising the left hand instead of rotating the right hand when a fish strikes. This will prevent excessive follow through, as well as speed up the actual motion by increasing your leverage. These things can apply to both light and heavy outfits, but are far more apparent in the latter. Finally, the heavy rod, being longer, is more difficult to carry assembled in your car or boat, for the tip seems either to stick out beyond where it should, or it is bowed considerably to make it fit into its proper space. So, in spite of their greater strength, heavy rods are broken just as frequently as lighter ones, since they are more frequently in jeopardy.

Rod "Actions"

Before leaving the subject of rods, I will emphasize

certain characteristics of action, that your rod, whether light or heavy, should embody. Referring back to theory, we have seen that the "flat spot" at the top of the wheel is of utmost importance, and that it is created by the bending and resultant shortening of the spoke. Now we are concerned with the possibility that the flat spot can be created more uniformly by a spoke that bends in a certain manner. Thus, a spoke that bends throughout its length will shorten more, creating a longer flat spot, which should be to our advantage. However, a spoke that bends throughout its length is more likely to bend most at midstroke, causing more concavity and resulting in more ruined casts. Obviously we are confronted with the problem of building a spoke that bends quite easily at the beginning of the stroke, but stiffens markedly from midstroke to the finish.

Some of the bamboo rod makers have accomplished this feat by building a rod that tapers quite rapidly from the tip to the middle, then quite slowly from the middle to the grip. When the stroke is begun, the soft butt section, in overcoming the inertia of both rod and line, bends quite readily at first, then refuses to bend farther, due to the resiliency of the material itself. At midstroke the stiffness and quickness of the fast tapering tip take over, after speed has been built up, furnishing plenty of force on through to the kill point. This is referred to as a "parabolic" action.

If you have never used such a rod you have a treat in store, for it will almost do your casting for you. In any event it is a feature worth considering in purchasing a new rod, whether light or heavy.

You are most likely to find this action in a bamboo rod, for most of the hollow glass rods sacrifice action for lightness, and too often the butt sections are of large diameter thin walled tubing, which flattens as it bends, losing, rather than gaining stiffness under extreme stress, for a flat tube bends easier than a round one. The more highly a glass rod is advertised for lightness the more likely it will be to fail in this respect.

GOOD FEATURES AND PROPER CARE OF RODS

In addition to proper action your rod should have a thread lock or spring lock reel seat, and though aluminum seats are attractively colored, and lighter in actual fractions of an ounce, all reel seats are located below the axis of the wheel, where weight is of no significance. It is a complete mystery to me that some manufacturer hasn't come up with a stainless steel or monel seat that will tolerate the first grain of ocean sand or dab of pumice without tearing the threads off or mangling the finish. The ferrules, for permanency, should also be of "hard metal" rather than anodized aluminum, for the same reason, and serrated, and with a moisture-proof partition, if your rod is bamboo. Guides and top should be stainless steel, carboloy, or monel to resist salt water, and the stripping guide should be carboloy (tungsten carbide). There are pumice areas in eastern Oregon where your line may pick up enough dust to become abrasive, cutting a groove in your tip guide in a single day, especially if you use the double pull, and it is a second mystery why no company has developed a light carboloy fly rod top that can be wrapped on.

If you would avoid ferrule difficulties, make plugs of soft wood that fit in the ferrule barrels. Let them absorb some light oil, or hot paraffin, and leave them in the ferrules whenever the rod is not assembled. They will prevent corrosion and exclude grit and moisture. The oil from your hair is salty, and should never be used on fer-

rules. Corroded or dirty ferrules can be polished out
with a wooden match stick, and though I am a nonsmok-
er, I carry a few matches for this purpose. In extreme
cases, twist a wisp of very fine steel wool around the
match, then blow in the ferrule after polishing to make
certain no residual strands remain inside.

A THOROUGHLY CLEAN ferrule will seat more
gradually and better if rubbed with a THOROUGHLY
CLEAN piece of paraffin wax. This is especially true of
anodized aluminum ferrules equipped with Neoprene
"O" rings.

Glass rods won't usually take a "set" from standing
in the corner (unless there is some abnormal heat
source), and I frequently use one-piece rods, or leave
others assembled the year around, because, until my
phone rings, I don't know which type of fishing I may
be doing next. But bamboo should be hung by each
joint, separately and vertically, if stored for the winter.
Never store any rod in a metal case for long periods.
Changes in pressure and humidity may cause a metal
case to "sweat" inside, causing strip separation and mil-
dew in bamboo rods and corroded ferrules or rusted
guides in others. Thus, any rod is shown greater respect
if hung in segments, and though it may seem like a nuisance at the time, it will seem like a "second Christmas"
when you take your weapons off the wall next spring to
start a new campaign of wits with your traditional adver-
saries (hopefully, fish rather than fishing partners).

So, assuming you have completed your "elementary"
fishing education, let's see what we can improvise in the
way of a "campaign" plan for the coming season.

IV.

THE CAMPAIGN

To those of you who have drudged through the preceding pages, practiced diligently, and obtained a degree of proficiency with your weapons (tackle) , the prospect of a campaign into an alien environment in an attempt to outwit and outmaneuver an unscouted adversary is perhaps the ultimate in contrast to the everyday monotony of the average career. Assuming that such a career permits a minimum of vacation time, the necessity of adapting yourself abruptly into wildlife habitat becomes correspondingly important. If you don't have a systematic approach, you may return home more frustrated than relaxed.

There will be many readers who have fished for many years; who have favorite lakes and rivers and seasons and riffles and flies and methods of approach. To these I would only say that after some forty years of guiding, and ten years of experiment prior to that, I still encounter days periodically when I wonder whether the favorable results we sometimes get are BECAUSE OF, or in SPITE OF, what we do.

So, feeling that I am not in a position to judge whether any person is right or wrong in a given situation, I shall again try to interpret, as nearly as I can, the things that I feel exist, are pertinent, and either advantageous or detrimental to fly fishing, leaving each of you to make his own "diagnosis."

INFLUENCES OUTSIDE THE WATER

Despite adequate evidence to the contrary, it is very easy to forget that influences above the surface of the water can affect a fish to a drastic degree. Frequently anglers, or even governmental agencies, may expect a fish to do something that under given conditions it may be nearly impossible for a fish to do. I have been guilty (and sentenced and condemned, too), for this misdemeanor of misunderstanding many times through the years, so I have known of its existence for a long time, but I had it accidently, drastically, and publicly driven home during one of my fly casting classes a few years back.

During such classes we practice out of doors when feasible, but when the weather is "impossible" we hold an indoor session with blackboard diagramming, questions, and answers.

THE "GADGET" EFFECT

In preparation for this I had devised a five foot glass tube, plugged at the bottom end, and filled with water to within a few inches of the top. Floating on the surface of the water was a "gadget" combination of lead sinker and toy balloon, with just enough air in the balloon to barely float the gadget.

The experiment was supposed to demonstrate the effect of changes in barometric pressure on a submerged, compressible object, such as a fish equipped with his all-important air bladder. By improvising a diaphragm over the top of the tube and pressing on it, the "gadget" could be made to sink, and by releasing the pressure, made to float again, thus duplicating changes in barometric pressure.

The demonstration worked fine until someone held the diaphragm down too long, whereupon the "gadget" sank progressively to the bottom and stubbornly remained there, regardless of how much vacuum was pumped at the top of the tube. And the toy balloon shrank until it hardly appeared to be inflated at all.

I was just as surprised as anyone at this unexpected phenomenon, and it isn't very flattering to realize that you have been fraternizing with a form of wildlife without understanding more of the basic problems.

Among conclusions to be drawn is the one that once a hatch of insects is over, and a surface-feeding fish decides to go deep, he isn't likely to come back for flies that come along just one at a time, so forget it. But at least the knowledge that this condition exists should make you more aware of the importance of hatches.

Other than by changes in depth, a fish's air bladder, at a given depth, will be contracted by a rise, and expanded by a fall in barometric pressure. Thus, when pressure drops, a fish may be encouraged to feed on the surface. Mother Nature helps the fish in this instance by decreasing the density of the air, causing newly hatched insects to flounder across the surface rather than fly vertically, for the same reason an airplane may require twice as much landing strip at an elevation of 10,000 feet.

For these reasons your best surface fly fishing may occur during periods of gently decreasing or at least steady pressure. If you have never owned a barometer, you may want one after reading this.

Not that fish can't be caught during high pressure; they can be. But bear in mind that you may be bucking bright light instead of overcast, strong winds rather than gentle breeze, insects blown into the water at random rather than hatching in a predictable location, and fish that probably won't rise to the surface from the bottom in more than three or four feet of water, for the simple reason that when they drop below a given depth they become heavier than the surrounding water, and in order to rise from there, they must "plane" up through the water, like an airplane taking off. Your fly has to look pretty easy to catch or they won't try to catch it, for the same reason you and I wouldn't try to catch a rabbit with heavy packs on our backs.

WATER TEMPERATURE

Before leaving the subject of a fish's buoyancy, the subject of water temperature should be considered. The gas which fills a fish's air bladder (which may or may not be air) may be expanded by a rise or contracted by a drop in the temperature of the surrounding water. Thus the detriment of rising pressure is often offset by a rising temperature as weather improves and the sun begins to shine; a situation that encourages some varieties of newly hatched insects to try their drying wings, and encouraging fish near the surface to remain there.

Water temperatures less than forty degrees cause most fish to become almost dormant, so you will usually be helped early or late in the season by sunshine or warm rain, or midday temperature.

All these influences will more drastically affect fish which have entered fresh water from the ocean, because their air bladders are developed to function in salt water, which has a greater density than fresh water, so they already have a "sinking" problem when they enter a river, thus, the "gadget" effect will be more extreme among ocean fish in fresh water. I am convinced that it has a direct bearing on the efficiency of existing fish ladders, for a fish with a collapsed air bladder, has a genuine problem, and in strange terrain they will avoid such risk if they possibly can.

THE THUNDERSTORM

Before leaving the topic of outside influences, there is one other phenomenon that merits some consideration, namely, the thunderstorm. The unusual activity of fish prior to such a storm has had worldwide verification, but the reasons behind such activity remain relatively unproven. It is true that there is usually diminishing light, for most such storms are preceded by sultry glare. There may be a warming trend of surface water, but often the weather will already be abnormally warm. There may be a humid condition in the air that might warn certain insects that the deadly threat of hail is pending, causing them to seek more adequate shelter. Or there may be combinations of these, plus the possibility that fish may be able to predict a pending period of "gadget" effect, resultant from the percussion of adjacent thunder.

However, this still doesn't explain, to my satisfaction at least, the behavior of fish at such times, for they will frequently hit any fly, regardless of size, color, or method of presentation, as if food were going out of style.

At such times, an examination of stomach contents will usually reveal a wide variety of insects, through the range of ants, bees, wasps, moths, beetles, crane flies, and occasionally even butterflies and dragonflies; insects not prone to fall in the water and drown without good reason.

This leads to an interesting theory—that such a variety may perish because they are possibly electrocuted before they fall in the water, or at least affected to a point below normal behavior.

It has been established that a goodly portion of the lightning strikes we see travel from the earth toward the sky, or at least meet halfway. Ground charges may form, and blandly wait for the cloud to approach before discharging, meanwhile loading every flying insect with a static charge of a given polarity. When the insect flies out of the area and over the river (which might furnish a ground to either plus or minus because of its mass and motion) he may be "whapped" just as you may be when sliding from a nylon-covered car seat.

No, I can't prove it, but a cryptographer would say that if its the question that fits all the answers you are getting close. Many of Nature's answers have been before us for countless ages, but modern Man is having a helluva time finding questions to fit them.

In any event, you will usually have superb fly fishing just before a thunderstorm, but there are some dos and don'ts involved for personal safety.

Do wear adequate clothing. A safety helmet makes a good rain hat, and is some protection during heavy hail, but an inverted boat is better, and your car is best of all. Don't ever park your car directly under a large tree; in case it is struck, a portion may fall. Watch the storm as it approaches, and count each time the lightning flashes. When the flash and thunder are less than five or six seconds apart, get in your car until they spread again.

Don't stay in a boat where you are the highest object for over fifty feet in any direction. Don't use metal rods or lines during an electrical storm, and don't stand closer than fifteen or twenty feet from a large tree, regardless of shelter, for lightning may jump from it to you if the trunk portion is dry. Never pitch a tent directly under a large tree during the thunderstorm season.

If lightning is striking consistently and close, lie flat on the ground if you are in open country, or lie flat in the bottom of your boat if trapped on a large lake. Absence of body beats presence of mind in this instance, so, unless you are braver than I, you will avoid it.

The kind of fishing that frequently occurs before a storm, makes it real easy to get trapped on a lake. I was in this situation once when lightning struck in the water within two hundred yards of our boat, raising a cloud of steam, but not touching our boat or motor, which were considerably higher. Since then I have felt like a fugitive from the law of averages. Don't duplicate my stupidity. And if you hear a noise of hissing, and "crackling paper," you are in a strike area. Just disappear completely for a while if you can.

Influences Under the Water—Rising Water

Before considering influences under the water that affect fly fishing, it might be timely to discuss the nature of the rivers themselves.

Most of our western streams are around a hundred miles long, heading at an elevation of some five thousand feet, and (in the cases of the McKenzie, Willamette, and Santiam) merging at a mere two or three hundred. Eighty percent of the drop occurs in the upper 20 percent of the distance, leaving roughly eighty miles of river with an average drop of ten or fifteen feet per mile. Most of the big rapids occur in the upper half, caused by massive ledges of rock, or boulders left where mountainsides have slid, but the lower half will have greater actual current volume as tributaries join at each successive intersecting valley. It will be broader, and most of the rapids will be replaced by "riffles," running over the gravel that has resulted from erosion.

A boulder, starting at the upper end, and moved by the power of successive floods, may have the corners knocked off in the first ten miles, may be ground quite round and just a foot in diameter when halfway down, and may be only the size of a marble when it finally arrives at the confluence. A roaring flood was required to move the boulder in the first place, but marble-sized pieces will roll at the slightest change of current, so channel change is occurring constantly in the lower portions of our rivers, sometimes even in midsummer. This is hard to discern from above the surface unless you know exactly what to look for, especially from such distances as Washington, D.C., where such erosion, causing channel changes, is apparently classified as "flood" damage by the Army Engineers (though actually accented by their practice of abruptly changing water levels at frequent intervals below almost every existing dam), possibly explaining why so many of their expensive revetments are a half mile from the nearest water. But a mobile riverbed is also quite a novelty to persons nearer at hand, especially novice fishermen. The noise of the constant percussion as your boat floats over a "traveling riffle" will make you think the king of all woodworms is eating the bottom out of your boat. Rolling gravel on the bottom makes a truly weird noise.

PERCUSSION

Naturally such percussion affects the activity of fish.

Many years ago (during my first childhood) I discovered I could obtain minnows for bait by locating a small isolated pool and slamming a large rock against a barely submerged rock in the pool. Any minnows in the vicinity were disabled by the concussion, and would turn on their sides, or belly up. Very few, however, would float, indicating their air bladders were emptied rather than ruptured by this percussion, for a burst bladder will usually cause a fish to float like a cork.

The indication that sudden percussion can cause an escapement of air from a fish's air bladder, whether involuntary (as in the case of the minnows) or voluntarily from fear, or to avoid possible injury or discomfort, has been demonstrated many times during the intervening years. I have had fine fly fishing ruined by everything from thunderclaps and jet planes breaking the barrier, to farmers blasting stumps adjacent to the river, and yes, I think, the first large rock in a given area to turn over with a loud "clack" as the power of rising water takes hold. The effect is identical with the gadget effect.

Adding to the discouragement of traveling gravel is the fact that its rolling dislodges numerous insect larvae upon which fish may be inclined to feed before the water becomes too discolored, so they can go through the period of muddy water and poor visibility on a full stomach.

As the water rises and becomes filled with sand and debris, fish stop feeding, for the same reason you do when you get the first big bite of shell in an egg sandwich. If you must fish during such circumstances, look for a large eddy where the "backwater" is traveling back upstream, then cover the back current before it rejoins the main current, or cover areas where water has flown through a clump of willows or other foliage. In the first instance the debris may have either sunk or floated. In the second, it may have been filtered out. Surface flies should be fished slowly, but with lots of action, and moved in contrast to the normal flow of debris so its motion contrasts when outlined against the sky.

Don't expect much of a bargain unless the water has been colored for some time, or is beginning to clear. In such instances fish may be hungry and ready to feed again.

HATCHES

"Hatch" is a term used by fishermen to indicate that insects are emerging from, or getting into the water in sufficient numbers to be of advantage to offer an artificial replica of a certain variety of fish food, thus becoming of possible advantage to a fly fisherman. Trout have "one track minds," often feeding on one type of insect at a given time to the exclusion of all others.

Many varieties of insects are not aquatic, and get into the water as victims of circumstance. The only reason for listing them as an underwater influence is simply that a sky full of insects does not necessarily constitute a hatch; only those that get in the water, and thus become available as fish food.

There are a number of possible ways to catagorize hatches. One might be by their origin; another by size, shape, or color; still another by their habits, abilities, or actions; or even a fly tier's problems in matching them.

AQUATIC AND TERRESTRIAL

Origin-wise, insects fall into two catagories; aquatic and terrestrial. Among the aquatics (insects that lay their eggs in the water) we can list the caddis, stone flies, and mayflies. These three in particular occur in an almost worldwide scope, and vary enough in their habits to be identifiable, even by novices.

A fly tier might designate the stone fly as a "flat wing," because the wings lie flat along the back of a rather flat body, like stacked lumber. Caddis (a green and gray version of which is known as a McKenzie locally) is a "tent wing," because their wings, at rest (if you can find one at rest), slope to either side, like the walls of a pup tent. Mayflies are "uprights" because they float on the water with their wings pointed toward the sky, like the sails of a boat, and sometimes fly in an upright position, for their wings are attached far forward on their bodies.

The term "terrestrial" would include any insect not established as "aquatic," and adds the shape referred to as a "fan wing" (though flying aquatics are also matched in this manner) and the shape of those insects having no wings at all.

FREAK HATCHES

The common, or "standard" hatches, referred to above, are predictable to a considerable degree, but there are a myriad of lesser hatches that the guide's "vernacular" would designate as "freaks." Trout will sometimes go berserk over some tiny inconspicuous bit of fluff that is impossible to match, and if you could you wouldn't be able to handle the weight and power of the fish you see rising with the size of hook necessary to match. Such insects may furnish some concentrated food supplement unknown to us, and evidently very important to fish, but the spectacle of such fish, feeding on such a hatch, is about like watching the President of the United States chasing a golf ball.

I recall being a member of a four-boat party several years ago when we had encountered such a hatch during the morning, and had stopped for lunch with nary a fish amongst the four boats. I had caught one of the minute insects (which hadn't been easy) and with public relations in mind, approached another guide whom I had met for the first time that morning, and inquired what he would call that particular bug, thinking, of course, of some commercial monicker.

He peered at it intently for a second or two, and then proclaimed: "I call any fly that size a damn nuisance."

Truer words were never spoken.

Among other "freak" hatches are spiders which feed a parachute-shaped web into an updraught, sometimes taking them many thousands of feet into the air. But when the wind blows instead, it can drag them across the water, like a water skier. Matching them can be a real challenge.

Another freak, known locally as a "scooter," which frequents the confluences of warmer tributaries, will, when newly hatched, "taxi" across the surface like a seaplane. So will crane flies, which resemble huge mosquitos. Mature scooters are parasitic, depositing their eggs on the bodies of other aquatic insects, which they bulldog in mid-air and ride into the water. During this hatch, you may need a "bi-visible" fly, one half to represent the dark scooter and the other half to represent the host insect, which is usually much lighter.

During "taxi" type hatches, a dry fly actually dragged across the surface at a steady speed will out-fish any other method, which may come as a shock to some dry fly purists. Think back to a time when some novice companion won all the bets.

Other freak hatches can be far too numerous to mention, but I remember a classic example several years ago on the lower portion of a local river. We had boated two or three miles, on a warm sunny day, and had stopped for lunch at a favorite gravel bar. Shortly we saw a nice fish rise in the riffle above, followed at regular intervals by several others, so we gobbled our lunches (our lunch being secondary to the fish's preference) and opened hostilities.

I suspected a hatch of drakes (a large mayfly, but dark and difficult to see), but several patterns didn't produce a symptom. Then we got into a "fly changing orgy" for two hours, without even a courteous refusal.

Finally, one of the fishermen saw a small fish rise and take something from the surface almost at his feet; an object he described as small, slender, and bright green, like a tiny bean pod. I tied on a small bright McKenzie (a hatch that had been over for two months) and we fooled the little eight incher. His stomach was full of bright green "tent caterpillars," about an inch long. We took a number eight Canadian sedge, trimmed it to a mere body, and proceeded to get a solid strike from every rising fish we saw during the remainder of the trip, but though I have carried such a pattern in my kit ever since, I have never encountered the hatch again.

The trout we tricked in the above instance were the profit resultant from alertness, persistence, analysis, improvisation, and I will readily admit, a considerable amount of luck. I think this combination furnishes incomparable recreation; something you can relive from memory, and I will guarantee that no member of that fishing party, on that particular day, will ever forget it.

Returning to "standard" hatches, there are still further divisions. Some may be referred to as "random," meaning that they may occur at any time, on any portion, of any river or lake. Others are "local," meaning they occur consistently in predictable areas of a stream or lake, and at predictable times of day or types of weather. I will attempt to give you a brief resume of the more common hatches, hoping it will help you to plan future "skirmishes" in your campaign.

STONE FLIES

I would classify the stones (locally misnamed caddis) as a "random" hatch, for the larva crawls above the water before emerging in the winged form and leaving the empty hull. Such hulls may be found on anything protruding above the water, and may vary in size from the "damn nuisances" to the huge salmonfly, sometimes almost four inches in length. They are unaffected by ultraviolet ray, and will sometimes crawl on, or flutter above the surface of the water in bright sunshine, but seem to prefer lesser light, possibly because, if you have a thousand eyes, you don't like to face all that glare without your polaroids.

The only predictable behavior occurs when the adults are ready to deposit eggs. At this time, they fly above, or hover over the water, occasionally touching it, frequently in the roughest portion of a heavy rapid, where feeding fish must snatch instantly or the opportunity will be gone. This is an ideal formula for fooling "old Grandpa," and more big fish are probably taken on a stone than any other local fly. Fish may show an interest in the stone at any hour, so it is probably the most consistent producer of the standard patterns, at least among random hatches.

CADDIS

Next to be considered among standard hatches is the caddis tribe, referred to locally as McKenzies, Mack Specials, or Cinnamon flies, depending upon color. The larva stage of this insect builds a protective hull for itself from sand, gravel, and twigs, held together by a tough membrane. These larva may be observed in almost any shallow pool, making you wonder if you need your glasses changed as you watch the oblong pebble, or watersoaked twig, crawl about on the bottom. Sometimes referred to as "rockworms" or "shell grampas," these larva can really upset your schedule, for trout love them, shell and all, evidently not minding the "grit" unless it is in a loose form that interferes with breathing. After a dose of "gadget effect," trout will frequently lie on the bottom and gorge themselves, disregarding your opinions, efforts, or epithets. A trout with his innards full of these can ruin the edges of your best knife, so beware of the "gizzard" on the first cleaning stroke.

When caddis larva prepare to hatch they crawl downstream to the first riffle below the pool they are in, emerge from their hull, and pop out on the surface like a greasy bubble, usually in the swiftest part of the riffle, and usually in "high gear and overdrive" when first appearing.

A caddis is probably the most active insect I know of, for he can duplicate, on the surface of the water, anything a cricket or flea can do on dry land, plus short "Quixote" flights in all directions almost simultaneously. Matching the size and shape of a caddis isn't too tough, but matching the action with an artificial is like trying to sneak a medicine ball into a game where a basketball is being used. In an effort to slow a caddis down, fish will frequently slap at it violently without trying to take it in their mouths, or arch high in the air from a distance of a couple of feet, planning to light on it from above. When these conditions occur you will get what you think are a lot of "goofy" strikes, not necessarily refusals. One netted fish out of five strikes isn't a bad percentage under such conditions, and most will be at your drop fly, which matches the action better, and doesn't mean there is anything wrong with your end fly. Incidently, this is one of the few instances when identical flies may be of advantage.

Sometimes caddis will hatch in mountain lakes, usually near the shoreline, so your longer casts may not produce until you have retrieved them quite close. In such placid solitude, a three- or four-pound fish, suddenly blasting the fly almost at your feet, will furnish a genuine incentive to "set" the hook. In my own case, the leader usually breaks. If it didn't the rod probably would, and if the rod didn't, my arm probably would, which might, at least, postpone the whole hideous ordeal until the following season. Professional football players may receive a hundred thousand bucks for risking a broken bone, so gambling on a mere fishing trip is ridiculous. I guess I must be plain addicted to caddis.

In any event, a heavy caddis hatch is a sight to behold, and if you haven't been through one you can't visualize the number of fish that can concentrate in a small area. The hatch occurs at about the same time every day, on almost every riffle, simultaneously, sometimes for thirty consecutive days or more, usually at midday on rivers, though morning and evening may be more productive on lakes due to light conditions.

The caddis is not affected by ultraviolet rays. I consider it definitely standard, local, predictable, and a joy to work with. After fish have fed on this hatch for a month they will weigh 20 percent more per inch of length.

MAYFLIES

Last of the major aquatic hatches is the mayfly. These also spend the larva stage of their lives under water and the winged cycle above, but whereas the stones and caddis may live for days or even weeks in the winged state, the mayfly may live only a matter of hours.

But creatures with short life spans have one inherent advantage; they have the ability to adapt far exceeding any of their neighbors, and I think the mayfly is possibly the most adaptable of any familiar form of wildlife. Eggs taken from an individual may, in part, develop into a larva that will crawl ashore and split up the back, like a stonefly, or come to the surface like a greasy bubble, similar to a caddis. Eventually I can dream of a situation when Fish and Game agencies may not only plant fish, but may also plant food sources that will help their fish plantings not only to survive, and thrive, but be more pleasurable to harvest by lures other than marshmallows or cheese. My number one candidate for this purpose, because of his adaptability, would be the mayfly.

PROBLEMS OF HATCH SURVIVAL

Of course, such plantings would be like casting pearls before swine unless a river is maintained under conditions in which larva can survive, but much of the damage being done is completely unnecessary.

As an example, I would cite an instance, some twenty years ago, when it became necessary to "spot spray" portions of the McKenzie watershed to control spruce budworm. I was on the river that day, and became concerned when a low-flying plane dropped some blobs of liquid into our boat from a tank he apparently thought was empty. When we reached the landing we went to the nearest phone and were informed that the planes carried a solution of DDT; that it was a contract job; that they would fly back and forth the cheapest route, which was over the river; and that though the route was over a portion of the river upstream from the city of Eugene water intake, it didn't make any difference because the tanks were empty and DDT was harmless anyhow.

The incident described above completely wiped out all aquatic hatches on a thirty-mile portion of the Mc-

Kenzie for three or four years, and it could all have been so easily avoided. But I fear this is rather typical of the average commercial layman's attitude toward "progress."

The other problem in making streams suitable for restocking with insects is the methods used in regulating the flow of water below existing dams. Frequently, such dams will change the water level below them from a matter of a few inches to sometimes a couple of feet. Some have reregulating dams below, to compensate for such abrupt changes, but too often the "reregulating" reservoir is kept at a constant level to facilitate powerboat launching and water skiing, with disregard for river levels below. Possibly persons in charge of such operations may feel that small salmon or steelhead planted or hatched a month before, should have learned to swim, and be self-supporting by this time, but the point overlooked is that such fish, in their development, depend almost entirely on aquatic insects and larva for sustenance, all the way to the ocean, which is sometimes a trip of several hundred miles.

Sadly, most of the persons in charge of such operations have never had the opportunity, as I have, to become acquainted with a "live" river, so they are unable to comprehend that on a normal rise of water, a larva will move toward shore, keeping out of the path of rolling gravel, but that if the water levels are zipped up and down like a yo-yo, he simply encounters a sudden earthquake, in the form of rolling gravel, which crushes him to bits, leaving nothing for posterity. More sadly yet, this procedure is completely avoidable, with no expense involved, merely meaning that water levels must be changed three or four inches per hour rather than ten or twelve inches per minute.

There are still a few "live" streams in Oregon, from which stocks of aquatic insects might be obtained, but they too are subject to "progress," in the form of impending dams, so, if you, the reader, are interested in an insect-stocking program, now is the time.

The Oregon State Game Commission has broken the ice with the stocking of some high lakes with freshwater shrimp, imported from Canada, for which I think they deserve a real vote of confidence. The stocking of insects on rivers would be a further step in the same direction.

Returning to the subject of mayflies, they are also unique in being one of the few insects that shed their skins a second time after emerging in the winged state. As a novice fly tier, I remember being startled when the jar full of March Browns I had brought home to match, had evolved next morning into a jar full of Red Uprights, and an equal number of empty hulls, which is still a good method of matching Red Uprights.

Mayfly hatches are a bit more difficult to match in the "field" than stones or caddis, for in rainy weather the hatch frequently occurs in deep water whirls and eddies, yet require a rather inert float to match properly, also requiring some technique, as well as your full attention, for the light may be poor, the naturals dull colored, and the maximum activity, coinciding with a heavy shower, the insects apparently sensing they are less conspicuous against the sky when rain causes surface turbulence. On squally spring days, I have seen half a dozen showers, and half a dozen corresponding hatches and lulls. But if you can get the "Indian sign," and match the hatch, you may net 80 percent of your strikes, with few, if any refusals.

Mayflies vary in size from "damn nuisances" to the two-inch "ecru" variety that hatches on coastal lakes and valley bass ponds, and vary in season from the "Pres-tone blooded" Blue Uprights I have seen in midwinter at ten above zero, to the "Bass" type that emerge on warm water ponds after a hundred-degree day.

Mayflies hatch on the lower portions of rivers early and late in the season, but in the upper reaches frequent-ly occur during the summer and at noon or early after-noon. The variety I am thinking of is a large insect with long gunmetal wings veined with black, and fairly vivid body color, in spite of which they are extremely difficult to see on crystal-clear turbulent water, and though they sometimes hatch in profusion, they emerge like bubbles, leaving no telltale hulls to indicate previous hatches. Watch for them in the slack behind a boulder, in whiter water than you thought a fish could live in, where your roll cast must instantly change to a rapid series of re-floats. All you need to do is handle the kind of fish you hook in such spots. Hah!

But, at least, you will feel their weight, and perhaps losing so many is really a conservation measure.

The insect described above was called a "black Cad-dis" in the early thirties; the more recent versions are called a Black Drake. It would be my first choice for stocking the white-water portions of rivers above all exist-ing dams. The biggest problem would be in obtaining stock to transplant, which might be like picking Moon-berries, but though I have never become adept at breath-ing water, I will volunteer if such a project is ever begun. This hatch may still occur in the upper portions of many of our rivers, unless governmental agencies, in the name of progress, have sprayed for mosquitos, or budworm, or tansy ragwort, or Canadian thistle, or poison oak, or face flies, or alder growth, or blackberry growth, or a thousand others which can be controlled by "specialists" better than could be done by individuals.

Being a midday hatch at higher elevations, this insect can be of real help to anglers who like to hike to the remote upper portions of our colder mountain rivers. I doubt if it would be adaptable to the warmer coastal streams.

TERRESTRIALS

Other than aquatic, insects must be classed as "random," or incidental, for such types get into the water by accident rather than intent. Important, however, is the fact that nature may provide many thousands of a given species when only a few are needed to perpetuate the race. This is never more true than in the case of winged ant hatches.

More important yet is the theory, supported by some experts in the field, that salt (possibly subject to "osmosis" escape from the blood stream of fish) is replaced in their metabolism by formic acid, an intoxicating substance, available to freshwater fish only in the form of insects that have a potent bite or sting. Backswimmers and mosquitos may furnish this item in lakes, but river fish are dependent on ants, bees, biting flies, and wasps, and possibly an occasional ant lion.

Therefore, after a winter "on the wagon," fish are acutely conscious of the first black ant hatch. The fiasco usually lasts about three days, starting when the first eighty-five-degree weather arrives each spring. The first day, trout will take the ant well, for no apparent reason, for you won't see many. The second day you may see ants, match them, and possibly have the best fishing of the season. The third day, ants will be crawling everywhere, including down your collar, at sunrise, but usually the melting snow from the previous weather will start gravel rolling, and the fish will be "stuffed," and on a formic acid "binge," and have a hangover for several days. So, after midmorning, you won't have much to work with.

In fishing the ant, it is imperative that a minimum of action be used, for this insect, once on the water, sticks like a postage stamp to the surface, in direct contrast to the "greasy" aquatics, so any action you give your fly will be to your disadvantage. Further, an ant on the water, though helpless, is far from being resigned, or subdued, thus, many small or medium, and sometimes large fish, are reluctant to take such a mouthful of buzz-saw and fire until the coals have been dampened for a while, indicating that the ant should be fished wet and dead. Try using a small, fluffy dropper for a "bobber," and setting any time it makes a sudden move. You will be right more often than you think.

In contrast to the aquatics, these insects apparently require ultraviolet ray, and warm temperatures, and are seldom seen in cloudy weather.

Ants, bees, and wasps are strictly random hatches, and though predictable to a degree, usually due to gusty wind, one spot may produce as well as another, but if the water is rising, and gravel starting to roll, try the slow, glassy flats, especially if you see fish rising.

MINNOWS AND STREAMERS

Your first reaction to the mention of "minnows" may be that they don't constitute an actual hatch, for they spend their entire lives under the surface, and don't progress from one stage to another except for gradual normal growth.

Nevertheless, minnows can have a direct bearing on

your fly fishing success, and are an absolute "must" in salt water, where winged insects are virtually unknown. I am convinced that minnows can be matched more accurately in size, shape, color, and action, by an artificial fly than by any other method. The possibly superior action of wood, metal, or plastic lures is more than offset by the disturbance made when casting, the lack of variety in smaller sizes, and the fact that you don't have to bring a fly all the way in to the rod tip to pick up and relocate over visible cruising fish. Under such circumstances, the fly rod will cover twice the area in half the time.

The term "minnow," actually a misnomer, is almost universally applied to small or immature fish of any species. In this group, anything from fry a half inch long to herring eight inches long may be duplicated, to "take" anything from perch and bluegills to cohoes, chinook, striped bass and albacore.

There is a negative "catch," however. Nature, always bountiful in reproduction, will again produce thousands of times the numbers necessary for perpetuation of the species. But whereas surplus insects may disperse over land areas, surplus minnows are all going to be in the water, so the fish you are seeking, being gluttons by nature, may glut themselves. Large bass, trout, and salmon may sometimes be seen cruising through such schools, taking a dozen at a mouthful, or maiming a hundred to be picked up at leisure. Apparently it isn't going to be easy to match a dozen minnows simultaneously with an artificial fly, so there doesn't seem to be any success formula for the poor starving angler in this instance. Still, case records will prove that sometimes fish can be caught at such times, but the reason has been attributed to "luck."

Luck, however, is a fickle entity, and lacks the consistency that records confirm. I had one lady fisherwoman who peered into the convex side of a hammered spinner blade. Seeing her reflection peering back from each segment, she concluded that the large fish hit it because it insulted them by making them feel like a group of adolescents. I'm not sure fish are sensitive enough to make this a logical answer.

But there is a logical answer, proven by a half century of case histories, on a worldwide basis, proving the effectiveness of such patterns as the Royal Coachman streamer, and other established streamers, among many varieties of fish. So we have the answer, but the question to fit this answer will vary almost as often as the number of fishermen involved.

To me, the most logical question was offered some years ago by a great naturalist, the late Gene Burns, in one of his fine syndicated columns shortly before his tragic death. Gene had established that fish, especially immature fish, as well as some larger fish, have the ability to change color to match their surroundings, sometimes in just a matter of seconds, thus camouflaging themselves.

I had often noticed that adult fish change color abruptly after death, like the magnificent albacore, whose iridescent glory fades to a lead gray, or the jellyfish, who spends his life rivaling the hues of a soap bubble, but fades to a colorless blob when he washes in on the beach. The full significance had escaped me, however, because it was so commonplace, proving that sometimes you can't see the forest because all the trees are in the way, and despite the fact that I had often taken pictures, when paper letters were stuck on the side of a fish and later peeled off, to prove that a customer had caught the "big one with his name on it."

Since Gene pointed out that the ability to change

color is more flexible in young fish, I can imagine they are often far better hidden than we dream of, thus, any minnow who contrasts with his surroundings instantly brands himself as a minnow with his "alertness" turned off. Whether from injury, carelessness, or inherited defect, he still becomes the target of any prowling predator. This is Nature's method of selective breeding.

So, it would appear that the artificial streamer that matches a hatch exactly will not be as effective as one which contrasts, fulfilling a novice angler's vision of paradise, and completely reversing the theory used in working insect hatches. Variation, however, in order to function at top efficiency, must still parallel the hatch to some degree. Obviously the variant you choose must be near enough in size and shape not to contrast in anything but color. Thus, if a school of minnows average three inches in length, a streamer fly half an inch long isn't going to be of much help, and vice versa.

Color variants likely show up in greater numbers during periods of fast-changing light; thus streamer angling may be more effective at dawn or dusk, especially in salt water. However, illness and death are no respecters of schedule, so a minnow may become ill or injured at any time of the day or night, but in addition, small fish, such as candlefish coming in to spawn, or fry of any species going out for the first time, may become confused by their first exposure to the "gadget effect," or by a change in the direction of tide flow, perhaps explaining the popularity of fishing tidewater areas at intervals of "slack" tide.

A troubled minnow, like many members of the insect world, will try to escape his torment by fleeing toward the strongest light, hoping his enemy will be blinded by the glare, or that the turbulence when he leaps and alights again above the surface will permit him to escape in a different direction, frequently resulting in the spectacle of a weakened minnow, with expanded air bladder, floating or swimming feebly, belly up, just under the surface. This would form the variant pattern most logical to match at random times, and you won't even have to know what the original looks like.

Those of you who have done skin diving, or viewed underwater gardens, will realize that a fish, floating belly up, will be reflected on the under side of the water surface like a mirror, contrasting with his surroundings like a torch in the dark. So, the top of your variant, representing the white belly of a troubled fish, should be white. The body and tail of the fly, representing the back and tail of the minnow, should be dark, but not necessarily identical with the backs of other small fish in the area. There should be some, but not too much red, for injured minnows in this condition have usually been exerting, and have possibly run out of blood, but there may be a wound, or a fragment of red gill showing behind the head.

Persons familiar with the pattern will recognize that I have just described a Royal Coachman Streamer. I doubt if it can be improved very much. The fly and its record furnish the answer. I hope I have offered a suitable question to fit its effectiveness.

No, I don't use one often, mostly, I suppose, because there isn't much to be learned that we don't already know. But keep a few in your kit anyhow, especially for salt water.

Before leaving the subject of small fish and variants, one more angle deserves attention. Most of us, at one time or another, have had small fish madly pursue some large lure almost to our feet, making us wonder whether he thought it was his mother, or whether he thought he was rich, or, more important, whether he was thinking at all. Thus, a grade-school youngster, though elusive as a caddis on the football field, may be caught easily when a fire truck is passing, or when his hand is in the cookie jar. I think this explains why small lures following a huge "lake flasher" are so effective, and why a drop fly or spinning bubble, ahead of your streamer, may take more fish than an isolated streamer, though in this instance your fly represents a curious or feeding minnow, so the color should not be inverted.

In addition, the turbulence caused by a retrieved bubble will effectively hide your white shirt, red hat, and waving arms. Of course this isn't really fly fishing, but if you are starving, it may be efficient.

FLY TYING

Many books have been written on fly tying, by persons of more agile mental and manual dexterity than I, but I feel obligated to touch on it briefly from a "do it yourself" standpoint. I think every fly in my somewhat ample kit is a direct result of a situation which I felt demanded a specific treatment. If you were to pick any one out, at random, I think I could recall the incident that was responsible for its creation. Fairly early in my "career" I discovered that you don't get rich in the guide business by following half a dozen boats, manned by guides of equal ability, then having your clients use flies identical with those the other fishermen are presenting. This basic truth, coupled with two common afflictions, ingrown indolence and chronic inertia, influenced me, following a brief period of exposure, to tie flies only for persons who fished from my boat. Besides, if you look too long at a given spot (like a fly vise) , you may develop into a yogi, which may be to some advantage, though I haven't seen many casting a fly.

Rarely does the food source I have attempted to match have a scientific name familiar to me, but many have been christened by my various fishermen. So, the big fan wing stone has become a "Hairless Joe" (with apologies to Al Capp) , and the same fly, in a flat wing style, was dubbed a "Drowning Collie," picturesque monickers, but hardly what one would attempt to catalogue.

A lack of technical information, however, should not be a deterrent to matching actual insects in the field, especially if they cannot be matched at convenient tackle stores. I think that improvised duplication, of actual insects, by your own two hands, is the biggest thrill of all. It has kept me in the guide business for forty years.

Inevitably, the question of whether fish are color blind arises at this point. To those who believe it I will answer that the best way to duplicate an exact degree of black and white is to match color exactly as we see it. No one can find fault with this procedure.

But, personally, I would go a little farther.

Flies may be tied in a variety of styles; in the case of streamers, the variety may evolve from the various materials from which the wing, which is the most important part of a streamer, is made. Flies duplicating a badly injured minnow might be duplicated by Marabou, which is only effective when retrieved very slowly, a panicked minnow, which may be duplicated with bucktail, or perhaps a larva which has no wing, but merely a "Palmer" hackle to represent legs. In all these instances, the argument might hold that such flies, silhouetted against the sky, become black. This might hold true for minnows, or insects with opaque wings, but what about those insects which have a transparency color in the wings, such as some of the mayflies, which are gray or brown if viewed from above, but may have a green or yellow cast when viewed against bright light from below?

My favorite example is a deer fly.

Those of us who have a distaste for wearing a shirt during summer, automatically become candidates for these green-eyed little monsters. We call them "flying Tigers" because they are striped man-eaters. Having one "sample," you, while in the middle of a tough rapid, where you can't drop the oars to "swat," is like bringing Pandora out of mythology.

But, this bug is fair fish food, being a midday hatch, in hot weather, awkward, and probably containing formic acid. Duplication has reaped quite a few limits, but if you think you can get the same results without putting a dab of fluorescent green in the fly to match the "tiger" eyes, be my guest. Personally, my experiences do not indicate that fish are color-blind. If they are, then the color adaptation of minnows is sure a lot of wasted time.

When making flies for your own use, rather than for resale, time is not much of an item. The most disgusting thing that can happen is to match a "freak" hatch, then have your only matching fly fall apart. This lends an incentive to use hidden knots instead of a tension, and to spare no expense in obtaining the best of materials for your own flies. Compared to "tailor made" flies, the price will still be nominal. I have flies in my kit that have taken a hundred fish, and are still serviceable.

LEADERS

Leaders are largely a matter of choice, regarding taper and breaking strain, but color can be of importance, and, in my opinion, almost as important as diameter.

The basic function of the leader is to furnish an interval between your lure and your casting tools, which isn't obvious when viewed from wherever a fish may be.

Therefore, in bright weather, a leader viewed against the sky should be blue; in overcast, gray or mist. If casting alongshore, under foliage, green might be the choice, but when fishing wet and deep, where fish see it in contrast to the bottom, it might be mottled, or olive, or whatever fits the situation. When fishing dry, a leader that matches the sky color perfectly may become useless if it becomes greasy and is supported by surface tension. Always dress your line and flies AFTER the leader and flies have been assembled, to avoid handling the leader with greasy fingers.

POLLUTION AND CONTAMINATION

The last items to be considered as influences under the water are the outlaws, pollution and contamination. Sadly, these influences originate above the surface, which dumps them right back into our own hands. Pollution, varying in form from sewage, pulp plant effluent, gravel plant mud, and sawdust dumps to road construction mud, road oil, logging debris which forms logjams, and crop or foliage dusting or spraying, have, in the past, destroyed wildlife, unnecessarily in many instances. Pulp plant mercury, radioactive fallout and offshore oil wells contribute.

THE "SANITARY LANDFILL"

Pertinent at this point is evidence that when dividing ownership of a cow, taking away the half that eats the hay (or taking away the hay itself) will stop the other half from furnishing milk. This can be equally true in instances where public relation "specialists," from large industries, "prove" to the public that their particular effluent doesn't kill fish, but it may be almost as deadly by destroying available hatches. Recently there is another threat on the horizon, in the form of a project, sold to an uninformed public, as a "Sanitary Landfill" method of garbage disposal. These are invariably located adjacent to a river that has enough flow to create gravel bars, where bulldozers can move earth more easily to cover garbage as it accumulates. Sadly, gravel bars are porous, permitting water to fill such pits at flood stage, and seep back out again when the river level drops. In a city the size of my home town of Eugene, with a population of a hundred thousand, I would estimate that the average family purchases and uses at least one can of insect pesticide per year. The empties (discarded pressure cans are rarely completely empty) are thrown in the pit, and crushed by a huge tractor with spike wheels, designed for the purpose. Then, the next time the adjacent river "floods," the water level in the pit matches the river level exactly, and when the flood recedes, the pit empties again, taking the pesticide with it, at a time when adult anadromous fish enter from the ocean, because temperature changes aren't as abrupt and rapids or falls are easier to negotiate. Likewise, small anadromous fish, going toward the ocean for the first time, will take advantage of the colored water and debris of a flood to help hide them from predatory chubs and bass and mergansers and herons. Both runs will be exposed to the full "benefit" of the pesticide, and according to President John F. Kennedy's Advisory Committee Report on the use of pesticides, published in 1963 (and still available at the Superintendent of Documents, Washington, D.C., 20402—price, 15 cents) , shrimp have been poisoned by concentrations as low as nine parts per

billion, which is a ratio of just a drop or two in an average swimming pool.

The most tragic part is that most pesticides are inefficient and unnecessary. For example, fleas and aphis
can be controlled by ordinary table salt, sprayed on in
solution, and, in the case of your roses, rinsed later with
the fine spray of your garden hose. And mosquitos, which
are the number one reason why the average person buys
a pesticide, are particularly vulnerable, to more simple
methods of control, being one of the few insects that
spend the larva stage under water, but are still required
to breathe air through a tube. If a larva can't breathe, at
the surface, for an interval of only a couple of minutes, he
will drown. I have taken a container full of mosquito
wigglers, poured a tablespoon of naphtha on the surface,
watched the wigglers die, and fifteen minutes later tasted
the water, which didn't have a trace of naphtha. (If you
don't like soup, leave the wigglers out). True, naphtha
is highly flammable, and other volatile liquids, such as
carbon tetrachloride, are either heavier than water, or
have toxic fumes, or both. But surely, among all the bril-
liant minds represented by successive graduating classes,
at various universities, there must be one capable of de-
vising a volatile liquid that is lighter than water, non-
flammable, and nontoxic, permitting the control of mosquitos without destroying other valuable aquatic insects.
To me, the use of the chlorinated hydrocarbon pesticides
is like shooting at a predator with a bullet that is going
to ricochet for ten years, threatening all other life in the
area. Every time I see a new sanitary landfill, I come
home feeling like a cougar had just walked across my
sleeping bag.

Frequently, when there is a possible choice between

whether disposal agencies or industrial influences destroyed something, they will point their fingers at each other and scream "I didn't do it, Mama; Joe did it," but fish or hatches are equally dead in either instance. My reason for pointing this out is simply that, if you enjoy fishing as much as I do, and feel that coming generations should be entitled to the same enjoyment, there is a degree of responsibility that goes with it. You, the average reader, are the only one who can insure that the "fifty-fifty rabbit sausage" of "progress" doesn't contain one horse for each rabbit, regardless of who screams loudest.

There may be many ways in which the "wool" of progress may be pulled over the public "eye." Industries that produce a popular, or perhaps even essential material or service, may have a "skeleton in the closet" in the form of radioactive, unsavory, or violently poisonous waste by-products. Some of these may be disposed of by placing them in underground tanks, admittedly a temporary measure. Some, prohibited by toxicity from being dumped in a river, may be sold to cities as a public water supply health measure so the city sewer system, which cannot be banned, conveniently dumps the poison into the river for them. Some by-products are periodically "accidentally" dumped at a hundred times their normal rationed volume, presumably by "inefficient" personnel. We had better hope that such employees don't lose their present jobs and pick up new ones with your municipal water system.

THE THERMOCLINE

Recently a plan has evolved to release water from certain dams to relieve a lack of oxygen (a bland way of saying that runs are being obliterated) which is a fine theory, but sometimes not ideal in practice because of some details (such as abrupt changes of river flow) , which are simple to control. But some others are not so simple. One that I consider a threat is a form of thermocline, which may cause the water released to lack oxygen.

Most encyclopedias explain the thermocline in considerable detail, including the density of water at varying temperatures, and whether a lake freezes; whether the wind blows, etc., but the problem I am thinking of deals only with reservoirs above dams (which aren't really "still" water) , and with water coloration.

It is common knowledge that, if you are critically ill, the hospital won't leave the beautiful flowers in your room at night, because most plants will release oxygen when exposed to sunlight, but will absorb oxygen during periods of poor light. This is part of Nature's way of controlling vegetation during various types of weather, preventing possible overgrowth and subsequent extinction of a species of plant.

But the same thing happens with underwater vegetation, causing the tragedy known as "winterkill" in high-elevation lakes, when too much snow covers the ice for too long a period, and which happened in my own little bass puddle here at home, just three years ago. Most of the big reservoirs, covering areas recently contoured, have a bottom of newly turned, fertile soil, encouraging the growth of an abundance of aquatic vegetation, thus almost assuring that, if the water entering at the top of the reservoir is colored, there will be an oxygen problem, below a certain depth, before it reaches the dam. Then, in most instances, water diverted down the fish ladder (if there is a ladder) is skimmed from the surface, which will have oxygen, but will also be warmer. Most anadromous fish, traveling upstream as adults, will prefer a colder tributary (which is what a ladder looks like to them), because colder temperature or salinity will retard growth of fungus. But what about the little guys, hatched from a previous run, going toward the ocean for the first time?

THE YOUNG MIGRANTS

Well, the first thing they may encounter is a quite liberal hatch of insects, for most such reservoirs are upstream from any heavy pollution (other than sanitary landfills) and will furnish enough food supply to tempt a small fish to remain, especially if he encounters a famine below, and is forced to return to the area to survive. If this situation occurs, a small fish may become a "native" rather than a migrant.

But in the event he decides to continue downstream, he will encounter other discouraging conditions. Most reservoirs have slack areas along the edges. The slack areas may develop a "bloom" of algae, or other vegetation, in an abundance that, though it may support insect life, darkens the water at a lesser depth, with the result that a small fish is still more inclined to stay rather than become anadromous.

But in the event he chooses the main channel instead, and drifts with it (in which event he won't realize he is drifting, having nothing stationary to compare with), he will arrive at the area, above the dam, where he may encounter a variety of conditions. First, if the dam is overflowing, he may be sucked over the lip (for he has no way of anticipating such a drop), and may fall a couple of hundred feet before he lights again. He may still survive this, unless he is in an area below one of the turbine tail pipes, which may be sucking water from below the oxygen level of the reservoir and have nothing left but carbon dioxide and nitrogen, whereupon our small fish, usually with a collapsed air bladder from the abrupt change of elevation, simply drowns.

His second hazard is that of being sucked down the turbine intake, which would be worse, adding compression and decompression to his other problems. His third possibility—he just might find one of the fish ladders and go down it, but the chance is rather remote, for the ladders are usually in a "fringe area," below vegetation areas, and if food is plentiful, he won't ever get that far downstream, and will become "landlocked," or "native" instead.

Of course he may be swept on downstream in midwinter if a violent flood occurs, but this is comparable to feeding your favorite hummingbirds too late into the fall, so that they may try to migrate after all the blossoms are gone, and consequently starve en route. A fish may do likewise.

But his fourth chance, and a very common one in power projects where there is a segment of canal between dams and the turbines themselves, is simply that he will follow the line of least resistance, and enter the canal, because most of the current goes there.

Here the warm surface water and any remnant of the thermocline will mix with good water because of turbulence, so that a small fish may drift peacefully along, at any depth, until he again encounters the threat of being sucked down a turbine intake. In this instance the current will be swifter, and though there will be a screening system of some sort, which might deter him temporarily, he will eventually have nowhere else to go.

Possible Ladder Improvement

This brings me to the point I wish to present; that it might be feasible to have both "upstream" and "downstream" fish ladders, one for the adults headed for the spawning areas and the other for the little guys going down. To most persons, a salmon is a salmon, and a steelhead is a steelhead, but in reality the contrast between the adult and the fingerling of either species is about as extreme as you can get in marine life, and when they chance to meet at a river mouth there can be a high percentage of cannibalism.

The "upstream" ladder might be most effective if the "intake" were taken from a strata of the reservoir containing the most oxygen, and colder than the surface, and it might be just a siphon even controlled automatically depthwise by photo-electric equipment, to coincide with varying color of the water in the reservoir. It should have sheltered "holding" areas at specific stages of elevation, where fish will feel secure while they adapt to the "gadget" effect, and it might be designed with a degree of "updraft" in such rest areas where these fish, who are heavier than the water they displace, might "coast" down hill and rest for a while, perhaps with a relaxed air bladder, without chafing their fins on the cement. I feel certain that such ladders would move fish over higher dams than has been accomplished previously, and might well be worth a try.

The "downstream" ladder, in contrast, might merely be a shallow spillway, without expensive holding areas if it terminated into any suitable site below that can be screened against predators, including herons, mergansers, and kingfishers. The problem isn't getting the little guys down; it's getting them to enter the spillway in the first place, before the turbines gobble them up.

But migrant fish are creatures with a high degree of built-in instinct, one branch of which is an inclination to shun darkness. In the instance of fingerlings, coming down for the first time, they might have gone too deep in the thermocline, developed asthma, and recovered again by fleeing toward the strongest light, but I'm inclined to accept instinct, rather than experience.

But adult migrant fish shun darkness too, proven by case histories where logjams have stopped runs, and one instance where a passage only twenty feet long, but apparently placed too deep, stopped an entire run of salmon at a small dam. Maybe they feel that any cavern that you can't see daylight at the other end of is going to be a "Jonah" type trip, and they don't feel as lucky as Jonah.

I think the screening above a "downstream" ladder should extend diagonally with the current, toward the spillway, should slope gradually downstream from, but uphill from, the bottom toward the surface, and should have screening too fine for fingerlings to penetrate, extending down to a depth of eight or ten feet.

Now, I wonder if a sheet of black plastic, fastened a few feet under the surface at the upstream end, and permitted to dangle in the current, like a flag flying flatwise, might furnish enough darkness to influence fingerlings to come in over the top instead of underneath? If such a contraption were only one tenth of one percent efficient, it still might be worth a try, especially if the spillway were well lighted at night.

Most of the items mentioned above might not be very expensive, but turbine intakes, adjustable to draw oxygenated water from varying levels of a thermocline, might be, and still should be included in plans for future dams, and installed in present ones where feasible.

In summary, the ideas I have presented here may be endorsed, questioned, or contradicted, which is fine, for an exchange of ideas helps win a ball game, but Mama Nature is referee of this league, and we won't win many by locking horns with this particular referee. Hippies may never conquer the earth, but they may inherit it sooner than we think. Last year there were over sixty thousand varieties of pesticides marketed.

And now I apologize to you, the reader, because the previous several pages didn't have much to do with casting or fishing an artificial fly.

Or did they?

Possible Help for a "Live River"

Still, at the risk of postponing your fish dinner, I feel obligated to explain one more point, namely, my reference in previous pages to a "live river."

This is a subject that should be approached gradually, for the problem involved developed gradually. Still, at the time you read this, it may have become another of Nature's answers, with the question to fit it characteristically obscure. It began way back when we first discovered that well water, polluted with typhoid, could be made safe by the addition of chlorine.

Chlorine thus became embraced as the ultimate in health insurance, and was considered an essential ingredient of soaps, and scouring compounds, and bathroom cleansers (and bleaches, where it may actually serve a purpose), as well as municipal water systems and sewage disposal plants, which is sort of like adding chlorine "fuel" to the chlorine "fire."

A point evidently forgotten is that any agent that will destroy dangerous microorganisms will destroy beneficial ones too, and some of the latter are essential, even in your own "innards." Most people are aware that such bacteria are destroyed by such procedures as the prolonged use of an antibiotic, or the excessive use of alcohol, but the medication can be discontinued, and the alcoholic has the privilege of guzzling buttermilk or yogurt along with guzzling booze. Even the guy on chlorinated water (and whatever goes with it to neutralize the taste) can take an anti-acid pill if he gets a reaction to the extra hydrochloric acid. But what about the poor defenseless river, adjacent to the average valley city sewage disposal plant, that gets all the chlorine, along with a myriad of other "progress" concoctions, shoved down its unsuspecting throat?

At about this point, the cougar walks across my sleeping bag again, for the same things that kill beneficial bacteria in our innards, will do it in a river too, the only difference being that if you or I were dead, somebody would notice it, but to the average layman, a dead river and a live river look exactly alike.

I wish there were a way of snapping our fingers, and making this ogre disappear, but I'm afraid it isn't going to be that simple.

There is a glimmer of hope, however. The first thing on the horizon is a "second look" at chlorine. Several years ago it was established that the effectiveness of chlorine depended upon its ability to offer, in dilution, an extra ion of oxygen, which accelerated the metabolism of microorganisms to the point that they died of "old age" before they could reproduce. This, apparently, is its only advantage, for experts in the virus field reveal that viruses, unlike microorganisms, don't really have a metabolism, and more nearly resemble crystal growth than animal or plant growth. Thus, chlorine is not a control, though the public has been led to believe that its use protects them against, for instance, polio or hepatitis. Most people would be thrown if they realized what percentage of the beautiful vegetables they buy at the average supermarket is fertilized with organic material originating at a sewage disposal plant. This might not be as spooky as it appears, for the best protection to date, against a virus, is constant mild exposure, again one of Nature's balances. If you get a strange one, though, from another part of the globe, like Asian flu, it can make you quite ill, in which event your doctor can't cure you; he can only help you recover. One lady in a local store recently was criticizing the policy of "keeping these nice Astronauts in a cage; they wouldn't dream of hurting anybody." I fear she has the terms lunar and lunacy associated a trifle too closely.

But even if an alien virus were brought back from the moon, he might be just as scared by the skinfuls of moisture and oxygen we represent as we would be of him. Or maybe the auto horns would scare him to death. In any event, chlorine wouldn't be the answer.

So, it would appear that instead of an ounce of chlorine being better than a pound of cure, we have been using more nearly a ton of chlorine to the pound of cure. The city of Paris, France, uses ozone (which offers the identical oxygen ion) but which is reputed to disperse readily from turbulence, leaving no acid residue in a river.

Sewage might be treated by heat rather than chemicals, cancelling viruses as well as bacteria. Sterile organic material in a river would soon be consumed by harmless bacteria and insects, which in turn would furnish food for downstream migrant fingerlings, as well as local trout. Thus, the control of chlorine, though only a single step, would be in the right direction.

Other steps are almost too numerous to mention. It is rumored that a prominent football coach, recently viewing his newborn eleventh child, expressed concern that there might never be an end. Compared with you and me, he doesn't have a problem. Suppose his firstborn had been a Frankenstein monster like DDT, and that during the ensuing twenty years he had seen sixty thousand others born, still without any possibility of an end?

There are several gruesome facets to be considered in the current use of pesticides. First should be consideration of an egg.

Those exposed to a mild dosage of biology will recognize that any egg represents a complete evolution of that particular creature, from a single-celled amoeba type on up to the present adult form. If there had been any tiny gap in the process, the species would have become extinct, and there wouldn't have been any egg in the first place.

Thus the connecting segments of development, representing many ages, cover a myriad of exposures and immunizations, which may have almost, but not quite, obliterated the species. When the next generation arrived they had to be immune to survive. This had to occur between generations, and it might have taken four or five to bounce back to previous numbers. This appears to be one of Nature's formulas, and applies to any form of life.

The spooky part lies in the fact that immunization, occurring between generations, favors creatures with short life spans, for they may be able to shake off something like DDT in five generations, during a single summer, while you and I, and our descendants, may pay, healthwise, for a hundred years. Whenever there is a positive in Nature, there is also a negative, however obscure, and we had better believe it. All too frequently, pest insects occur in cycle years, sometimes in quantities requiring some kind of treatment, but use of the average pesticide first results in the destruction of any natural control creatures, which get an overdose by eating poisoned pests and which usually don't occur in cycles, and have longer incubation periods, leaving no choice but more pesticide the following year. Of course you can get one of the recently more potent pesticides. Or you can use several times more DDT. But the DDT monster broke down, didn't he? Yes, he may have broken down on the flies and mosquitos. But he may not be through with you and your family for ninety-nine more years. Still, on the very year of your problem, without interference, Nature might have compensated. I read in a book somewhere a quotation that said: "Ye of little faith."

A portion of the problem lies in the hands of those persons, whoever they may be, who encourage spending half a lifetime of drudgery in obtaining a specialized education, only to find that, due to political manipulation and governmental budgeting, there is only one available job for forty or fifty applicants, and that job shackled by a "slave contract," meaning that anything developed in research, by request or otherwise, becomes company property. Dollar marks may command respect now, but there must be life, before dollars (or whatever medium of exchange is developed next) can be appreciated.

So, the winner gets a slave contract. But the losers?

Well, the losers get to develop some "manual skills" like digging ditches, or harvesting crops, or driving taxi, or scrubbing floors, or, if they get hungry enough, washing dishes. Some of the lucky ones may already know carpentering, or plumbing, or plastering or mechanics. In any event, I think the future lies this time in the hands of the "losers." There is prophecy indicating that the meek shall inherit the earth. From where I stand, these guys who have tried their best, been beaten due to influences beyond their control, and struggled back in another field, represent the "Meek." I won't be around to complain fifty years from now, but if ten million healthy humans inhabit our planet then, they will be from the ranks of the Meek. Meanwhile I hope the "losers" help bring a few rivers back to life rather than creating any new monsters to mangle our ecology. I am confident they have the ability to do either. I give them my vote, and wish them luck.

There is also prophecy predicting the eventual appearance of an entity referred to as the "Anti-Christ." One interpretation might be that the population of a planet, discontented with their present lot, still may not be quite smart enough to take the manager's job. Total content is an abomination, for it leaves nothing to lead us forward. But leaving "footprints on the sands of time" without regard to where they lead, or where they may lead others, is not the answer. They just might lead to a situation where there might not be anyone to make footprints.

DRIVING ALERTNESS

The final item I offer, prior to your fishing skirmish, is of a more immediate nature, merely an urge to maintain alertness en route to the fishing area. Most western rivers flow from east to west, meaning that if you travel upstream in the morning you may be facing a glaring sun, and if you return in late afternoon, you will be facing it again. At such times, a spot of chrome on the dash or hood, a bit of dust or film on the windshield, or even polished wax on the hood may accent your visibility problem.

I am sure the average driver realizes this. Still, because he may be preoccupied, going to or from work, it is rare that an oncoming driver will turn on his headlights, even when passing another car in your lane. From his viewpoint, with the sun directly on you, you loom up like a mouse in a pan of milk, and he may not realize that he could be completely hidden.

Eventually there will be a law requiring that a vehicle be equipped with lights that turn on automatically whenever it is in motion, instantly identifying one with white or green as coming toward you, and one with red as going away, as well as making their distance from you obvious. Until then, I think it is a good "rule of thumb" to look in your rear-view mirror, which is exactly what the oncoming driver sees. If the background color matches the paint of your car, he may have turned on his lights in an attempt to prevent you from becoming another of Nature's answers, referred to as a "vital statistic."

But, for now, let's stop worrying, grab the fly rod, crank up the old hack, turn on the headlights, and live a little.

V.

THE SKIRMISH

IF YOU HAVE followed the devious path through the hopefully logical campaign influences of the previous pages, you are probably more than ready to engage the opposition in a contest, with a bonus of a fish dinner if you are the winner. Perhaps I can eliminate a few battle scars if I outline approximately what I do prior to such an encounter.

WEATHER REPORT

Beginning the previous evening, I listen to a weather report. If the weather is to be cool and rainy (common at the beginning of the season) I expect the fly fishing to be best near midday, when air and water temperatures are at greatest contrast, otherwise there is no incentive for an insect to hatch, for his wings won't dry enough to permit him to fly. Probably the insect of best advantage will be a mayfly of some sort, because they are already in midstream when they emerge, thus, rising fish will be more obvious. Insects hatching near, or on, shore will likely cling to the underside of a leaf until the temperature and humidity improve. Most artificials should be fished dry and "dead," because insects won't be very active.

If the day remains soggy and cold, nymphs are your best bet, especially if the rain is heavy enough to affect the water level. Try spots where the gravel would first begin to roll, for a shallow riffle, of small gravel, will move first, dislodging nymphs and larva that would otherwise be bedded down. Hungry fish will pick a spot where they can see the surface from the bottom, regardless of the color of the water, because, in colored water, they can best distinguish food from debris when it moves, outlined against the sky, in contrast to the normal flow of current. Under these conditions, don't be surprised if you take a good fish where your hip boots and flat feet would normally be. Work the fly in contrast to the current.

A HATCH EXAMPLE

If the weather begins to break, and the temperature rises, mayflies may come out in hordes, and you may have action for a while, but if you see larger flies hatching, such as stones or caddis, the larger fish may prefer them later in the day. This phenomenon is referred to in the guide vernacular as a "switch in hatches." I've had it happen four times in a single day.

If the weather is wet and soggy, but still and warm, caddis will usually appear, though stones, cranes and scooters are a possibility, and the second stage of mayfly, referred to as Imago, may be of advantage. Fish rising in glassy "slicks," or eddy foamlines, indicate mayflies; along overhanging brush, stones or cranes, or yesterday's caddis, at the mouth of a warmer tributary, scooters, etc. Sometimes at dusk, the mayfly Imago can become a real "Amigo," for fish may be taken by merely trailing a fly behind the boat, which sure helps on a tough day with tired novice fishermen.

If the weather is warm and still (usually indicating a steady or falling barometer) fly fishing should be good, including a variety of patterns, and the possible advantage of a thundershower if the weather "over-improves."

If the day becomes hot, and the pressure rises, sur-face hatches may fly into the sky immediately upon emerg-ing, and thus be of little value for numerous "takers," but you might fool Old Grandpa in a spot where he would need to hurry. However, on most such days, a heavy afternoon wind develops, blowing insects into the water that normally wouldn't be there, and offering you an unlimited variety to experiment with, though, of course, with coincident casting problems.

One of the possibilities on a hot windy day is the lowly grasshopper. I well recall a trip to Wickiup Reser-voir, on a "postman's holiday," more years ago than I like to remember. I think it was about mid-August that I drove out on a barren promontory and started casting at midday, on a hundred-degree day, with gusts of wind possibly to fifty miles per hour, moving heavy bursts of dust, and sometimes small pebbles across the landscape. Under such conditions, no one in his right mind would even think he was fishing.

But a herd of Whiteface cattle had wandered down to the water to drink, and as I watched, a tremendous fish rolled, fifty or sixty feet offshore, and then another, and another.

Thinking I had located a school of "minnow feeders," I proceeded to the area, whereupon the cattle moved on. I tried a streamer for ten minutes or so, without success, and without seeing any other rises. Then, directly off-shore from the cattle, there was another swirl that looked like a whale had spouted.

At about this point, I began to hold a council of war with myself. For many years there has been a degree of public opinion voiced, comparing the attributes of pro-fessional guides with areas recently vacated by bovines.

Under these conditions it doesn't bolster your ego when you discover you are playing "second fiddle" to a herd of cattle, so I circled them at considerable distance, and cut in ahead.

The first thing I noticed as I proceeded along the shoreline was a yellow-winged grasshopper, which tried to fly, was caught by the wind, and blown some fifty feet out into the water. He kicked vigorously several times, with folded wings, and then disappeared into the maw of a lunker trout.

I think it is normal, at such times, to succumb to a degree of palsy while you scatter the contents of your fly box. Hoppers are not a standard item in McKenzie River fly boxes. I finally settled for a No. 6 flat wing Stone, smeared the wing solid with Mucilin (line dressing) and semi-rolled it out about fifty feet. At about the third kick, yeah, you guessed it.

The bed of Wickiup is a mess of stumps, and in some cases, entire small trees. You don't land every fish you hook, and I recall losing five flies in fish that day, but I also landed enough in two hours, to fill adequately the legal limit of fifteen pounds and one fish, including a Brown over nine pounds, a couple of hefty Rainbow, and one four and a half pound Brookie. It's pretty easy to get carried away on that kind of a day with surprise conditions, and fish larger than you are accustomed to, and when I got back to camp, I began to wonder what on earth a lone guy, on a three-day trip, could possibly do with that much fish, when he couldn't eat over half of one in that period. So, I cranked up the old hack and came home, and froze the fish in separate cakes of ice, and thawed and ate them at intervals for a couple of years.

But I've never been back to the spot. Why? Because every time I thawed one of those fish, I got sort of sick, recalling the whole episode. I had been given the "Indian sign," and I had misused the privilege. Maybe in this instance it didn't make much difference, for an "improved" dam now increases water area, and changes water levels more rapidly, obliterating spawning areas as well as the hopper population, but that isn't really any excuse, and I'm not too proud of that portion of history. On that day I could have killed, and wasted, a hundred pounds of trout.

Oh, I've been back to Wickiup many times, but I shun that portion. I think it's because it's too much like visiting a cemetery. Let's hope our current fishing areas don't evolve into cemeteries, and that we, personally, don't contribute in the event they do.

Hoppers will float quite a while unless the water is exceptionally rough, so you will likely see rising fish, and the same is true of other buoyant or surface hatches, with the type of insect indicated to some extent by the location of the rises, establishing a "pattern" to work from. If you get a pattern going, stay with it till it quits you, for some may last through your entire vacation period.

Matching Random Hatches

Random hatches may not be so simple however, for the fish may not be patronizing a given area in unusual numbers; still, they may clobber the feathers off a certain fly in preference to all others. If you can establish a working pattern on a random hatch, it is like striking gold, for it permits the use of isolated areas where other fishermen won't create a crowding problem. Of course there isn't anything wrong with telling everyone all about the fly that is doing such good work for you. You can also give them your favorite book, and say "Here's a mystery you will really enjoy; the butler turns out to be the killer." I usually don't do either unless some poor guy is in the throes of a genuine knowledge famine.

Well, that's about the way the average guide plans a skirmish. But do these plans really work? Not as often as I would like.

However, they will get you out on the "playing field," where you can see which way the ball bounces, if and when it bounces. Catching it is a personal problem.

A Point for Consideration

In closing, I would point out once more that the artificial fly is the deadliest of all lures; that the thrill lies in outwitting an alien creature in an alien environment, not in wanton slaughter, and that if you can consistently deceive the largest fish you see rising on a given day, you won't feel the urge to boast, because the fish will already have presented you with the ultimate compliment.

I wish you tight lines and happy days.